FIT FOR PURPOSE

Become a Living Vessel God Can Use

Beyr Reyes

INTRODUCTION

Have you ever been driving along at midnight and hit an unexpected dense fogbank? The road lines vanish depriving you of any guidance. Lights bounce back into your eyes, blinding you with your own attempts to light the path. Speed feels suicidal, yet stopping feels like dying in place. Every reflector is a trick. Every shadow is a deer, oncoming semi, or cliff. You grip the steering wheel hard and proceed despite the fear and uncertainty, because you know the only way out is through.

Have you ever hit a fog bank in life? It feels like that same midnight drive but can last for months or years. You wake up every day in the haze. Familiar roads like marriage, career, school, ministry, and health disappear ten feet ahead. Goals, dreams, and even your own identity turn the color of wet cement. Prayer feels like talking into your pillow. Scripture reads like someone else's mail. Other people's lives speed past in clear weather while you crawl along, high beams on low, terrified of making a wrong turn.

Fog banks and other wilderness seasons come and go in our life, just like fair-weather times. Maybe you're not fumbling through an uncertain season but can see clearly where you need to go. Maybe you have a distinct vision ahead but just don't know how to get from here to there.

We all have a purpose in life and drive towards it every day whether we can see it or not. Before we can see our purpose clearly, sometimes we need to get in shape to fulfill it, and other times we need to get fitted for it. In other words, sometimes we need to shape ourselves to fit our purpose by preparing ourselves in body, mind, and skill. Other times, God must fit us for it, using struggles, detours, or unexpected shaping, so that we're aligned with His larger design.

God shapes our lives much like a potter forms clay on the wheel. He presses, stretches, refines, and sometimes reshapes us. But we also have a role in that process. We must not only submit to His shaping but actively pursue growth and alignment with His will. *The goal is to become a living vessel to carry His purpose without leaking, so that what He pours into us can be poured into the lives of others.* Becoming fit for purpose includes what we do for ourselves in addition to what God does to us.

What does "fit for purpose" mean to you personally?

If God were to ask you to do something, could you? Would you have the physical health and fortitude? Would you have the time? The finances? Would you have the skills and knowledge to accomplish it? Do you know the right people? Are you in the right headspace?

WHAT IS PURPOSE AND WHO HAS IT?

Let's just jump right into the fire and first address the age-old question:

Why am I here?

The short answer is—because you have a purpose to fulfill.

Yes, everyone has a God-given purpose. It may not always look the same (or unfold on the same timeline), but the Bible consistently affirms that no one is created by accident.

> *For we are his workmanship, created in Christ Jesus for good works, which God prepared beforehand, that we should walk in them.* EPHESIANS 2:10 ESV

> *"For I know the plans I have for you," declares the Lord, "plans to prosper you and not to harm you, plans to give you hope and a future."* JEREMIAH 29:11 NIV

Everyone who is called by my name, whom I created for my glory, whom I formed and made. Isᴀɪᴀʜ 43:7 ESV

But now, O Lord, you are our Father; we are the clay, and you are our potter; we are all the work of your hand. Isᴀɪᴀʜ 64:8 ESV

The Lord will fulfill his purpose for me... Psᴀʟᴍ 138:8 ESV

Every person is uniquely designed, with good works already prepared for them. This was originally spoken to Israel in exile, but the principle applies broadly: God has intentional plans for His people. At the most basic level, our purpose is to reflect God's glory through our lives.

But what really is purpose?

Some purposes are universal (to love God, love people, live for His glory). Others are personal and unique (specific callings, assignments, seasons of impact).

At its core, purpose is the intersection of three things:

- *Calling* – what God intends for your life (the bigger, spiritual "why").
- *Capacity* – the unique gifts, strengths, and experiences you carry.
- *Context* – the season of life, opportunities, and people around you right now.

Purpose is not always one single "life assignment." When we think about someone having purpose, the first things that come to mind are pastors, TV evangelists, Sunday school teachers, nuns, etc. You know—the people who devote their entire existence to a single cause. This autopiloted thinking is a design from the enemy to make us think that if we aren't like these people, then we don't qualify as having purpose. It's a lie.

Just because you're not devoted to a single cause does not mean you don't have purpose. Purpose exists in layers, and like an onion, each of us have them.

We all have a *lifetime purpose* to love God, love people, and reflect the character of Jesus. This never changes and stays with us from birth to death. It's a general pursuit for every second of our life, and it should permeate and direct every single action we take.

Seasons of purpose come and go in our life and include times for things like raising children, building a business, serving a community, or caring for a loved one. These could last for months or years and require us to focus our attention and energy on something in particular.

And then there are *moments of purpose*. These are specific assignments like taking a ministry trip, comforting someone God lays upon your heart, or sharing your testimony with someone who needs to hear it. We rely on the tug on our hearts, eyes, and ears to become aware of many of these occasions.

Why is purpose so hard to pin down?

Purpose is hard to pin down because it's not static, it unfolds. It's less like a single destination and more like a journey of being shaped and prepared. Following are the main struggles when it comes to finding purpose.

- *We tend to think too big, too soon.* Many people assume purpose means one giant, lifelong mission. In reality, purpose often unfolds step by step with one "yes" leading to another.

- *We compare ourselves to others.* It's easy to feel like we don't measure up when we look at someone else's calling. But their purpose fits their design and season, not ours.
- *We expect clarity without preparation.* Sometimes God doesn't reveal the full picture because we aren't prepared yet. Seasons of training and shaping clarify what we're meant to do.
- *We confuse identity with assignment.* Our identity is constant (beloved, chosen, valuable). Our assignments shift over time (parenting, career, service, leadership). Mixing them up leads to frustration.
- *Fear and doubt cloud our vision.* Even when we sense a nudge toward purpose, fear of failure or lack of resources convinces us we've heard wrong. Purpose gets buried under all the "what ifs."

The difficulty of defining purpose is exactly why this book matters. Oftentimes, we only see our purpose in hindsight, looking back and realizing how our discipline plus God's shaping worked together, whereas this book helps you recognize it while you're still becoming.

Why do some people know their purpose and others don't?

We all move through lifetimes, seasons, and moments of purpose, and at least two of those are happening at any given time. But in a culture hooked on instant gratification, it's easy to forget that. We overlook our lifetime and seasonal purposes and zero in only on the "moments," then judge our whole lives by whether we're experiencing those quick hits of meaning. When they don't show up often enough to satisfy us, we call ourselves failures.

Some people seem to "know" their purpose because they've learned to pay attention. Over time, they've trained their ears and hearts to recognize God's direction in both the quiet seasons and the urgent moments. Others struggle not because they lack purpose, but because noise, hurry, and misplaced expectations drown it out. Purpose isn't hidden from a select few; it's revealed through attentiveness, obedience, and faithfulness in small, often unremarkable moments. When we stop chasing constant affirmation and start listening, clarity tends to follow.

Sometimes the reason someone doesn't "know" their purpose is because they're not yet fit to carry it. God, in His mercy, may withhold something until the person has developed the strength, character, or discipline to handle it well.

And then, there are those people who do have a sense of their purpose but dismiss it because it feels too big, unrealistic, or risky. Fear, doubt, and unbelief can bury purpose under layers of excuses: "Not me. Not now. Not possible."

Sometimes God reveals purpose gradually to protect us from pride or shock. If we saw the whole picture too soon, we might either run ahead in our own strength or collapse under the weight.

Do you ask God every morning?

God gave us a user manual for this thing called life, and inside it, He says to ask and you shall receive. Are you asking, first thing every day?

Ask, and it will be given to you; seek, and you will find; knock, and it will be opened to you. Matthew 7:7 ESV

Following is a prayer I pray every day. Feel free to use it.

> Lord, quiet the noise around me and within me. Open my eyes and ears so I can know Your voice today. Order my steps, sharpen my discernment, and help me recognize the purpose You've placed in front of me. Give me the courage to obey quickly and faithfully.

WHAT IS FITNESS?

Imagine you're on the lightning round of Family Feud. Top five answers on the board.

"Name a way someone would define fitness…"

I'm betting that most people would say something like "being in good shape."

And I'll double down that if you asked them to gesture what fitness looks like, they would flex their biceps.

Am I right?

Fitness does mean "being in shape," but that's only part of the picture. And fitness isn't the same thing as athleticism, no matter what all those magazine covers suggest.

The most general and all-encompassing definition of fitness is "the state of being fit."

What does it mean to be fit?

When we describe something (or someone) as being fit, we are generally referring to it being of the right size or shape, being suitable or appropriate, having the right qualifications, being in good condition, and being proper or worthy.

Being "fit" goes beyond any single definition. It's a combination of qualities that allow a person, object, or system to function well in its intended context. Understanding this broader view of fitness lays the foundation for exploring the many areas of life where we can strengthen and grow ourselves intentionally.

What are important types of fitness?

Let's start with the most recognized type of fitness: physical fitness.

Physical fitness is the physical ability to effectively perform tasks and activities involving strength, endurance, flexibility, and cardiovascular health. Some key components of physical fitness include:

- The ability of muscles to exert large and/or explosive force.
- The ability of the body to sustain activity over a prolonged period of time.
- The range of motion and flexibility in joints and muscles.
- The efficiency and performance of the heart and lungs during activity.
- The body composition of fat, muscle, and other tissues.

Other types of fitness, however, are equally important and often overlooked.

Emotional fitness is the ability to understand, manage, and use your emotions in healthy, constructive ways (especially when life gets stressful or uncertain). Someone who is emotionally fit tends to:

- Recognize what they're feeling, in the moment.
- Regulate their reactions and not let emotions like anger and sadness control their behavior.
- Bounce back from setbacks (emotional resilience).
- Maintain perspective and avoid spiraling into worst-case thinking.
- Communicate their feelings clearly and compassionately with others.
- Make choices guided by both wisdom and emotion, not just impulse.

Spiritual fitness is the capacity to live with a sense of meaning, alignment, and inner grounding, and to let that sense of purpose guide your choices, relationships, and responses to life's ups and downs. Spiritual fitness isn't about perfection or never doubting. It's more like having a compass you return to, something steady that helps you orient your life, grow through challenges, and love people well. People who are spiritually fit typically:

- Know what they believe and value (and try to live in line with it).
- Feel connected to God, faith, community, creation, or something bigger than themselves.
- Find meaning in hardship, instead of seeing pain as pointless.
- Practice reflection (prayer, meditation, journaling, worship, etc.).
- Act with compassion, integrity, and gratitude.

- Have hope and direction, even when circumstances aren't ideal.

Social fitness is the ability to build, maintain, and navigate healthy relationships, and to function well within families, friendships, workplaces, and communities. Social fitness isn't about being outgoing or having a huge friend group. It's about having the skills and habits that help relationships thrive and being able to rely on (and be reliable to) others when life happens. Someone who is socially fit generally:

- Connects with others and forms supportive relationships.
- Communicates clearly and listens well.
- Resolves conflict constructively instead of escalating it or avoiding it.
- Shows empathy and respect for differences.
- Contributes to community, not just themselves.
- Knows healthy boundaries (what to say yes/no to).

Intellectual (or educational) fitness is the ability and willingness to keep learning, keep thinking critically, and keep applying knowledge in everyday life. It's less about how many degrees you have and more about having a growth mindset and about being teachable, open, and mentally engaged with the world. A person who is intellectually fit tends to:

- Stay curious and ask good questions.
- Seek out new knowledge or skills (reading, training, courses, problem-solving).
- Think critically and evaluate information instead of just accepting it.
- Make informed decisions based on evidence and reason.
- Adapt and learn from mistakes.

- Use what they know to solve problems, create, or help others.

Occupational fitness is the ability to engage in work (of any kind) in a way that is sustainable, skillful, and supportive of your overall well-being. It's less about status or title, and more about being able to function well in whatever work you're called to do, whether that's paid employment, caregiving, volunteering, or running a household. People who are occupationally fit generally:

- Develop the skills their role requires and keep improving them.
- Show reliability and responsibility in whatever work they do.
- Manage time, effort, and stress so work doesn't overwhelm their life.
- Find healthy motivation and purpose in their tasks.
- Stay open to learning and adapting when roles or expectations change.
- Build and maintain social networks for learning, mentoring, collaboration, and career/role development.

Financial fitness is the ability to manage your money wisely, so it supports your needs, goals, and long-term stability instead of being a source of constant stress. It doesn't mean being rich. It means being steady, intentional, and prepared so money supports your life rather than running it. People who are financially fit typically:

- Know what's coming in and going out (they track spending and income).
- Live within their means and avoid unnecessary debt.
- Save consistently for emergencies, future goals, and big expenses.
- Plan ahead (budgeting, insurance, retirement, etc.).

- Make thoughtful decisions about spending and investing.
- Use money as a tool, not as their identity or source of worth.

Time-management fitness is the ability to organize, prioritize, and use your time effectively so you can accomplish what matters most while maintaining balance and avoiding burnout. It's about making your time work for you, so your energy, attention, and actions align with your goals and well-being. People who are time-management fit typically:

- Plan and prioritize tasks based on importance and deadlines.
- Set realistic goals and break them into manageable steps.
- Use time intentionally, minimizing distractions and procrastination.
- Balance work, rest, and personal life to stay productive over the long term.
- Maintain flexibility so they can be available for unexpected needs or opportunities.
- Adapt when schedules change, maintaining focus without stress.
- Review and improve habits to continually make better use of their time.

There are many other types of fitness, but the ones mentioned herein are the focus of this book.

WHAT DOES IT MEAN TO BE FIT FOR PURPOSE?

According to the online Cambridge Dictionary, fit for purpose means to be:

Suitable and good enough to do what it is intended to do.[1]

According to the National Institute of Standards and Technology (NIST) Computer Security Resource Center:

Being fit for purpose requires suitable design, implementation, control, and maintenance.[2]

But how does God define it?

...so that the servant of God may be thoroughly equipped for every good work. 2 TIMOTHY 3:17 NIV

---

[1] Cambridge Dictionary. (n.d.). *Fit for purpose: Definition.* Cambridge university press. Retrieved December 29, 2025, from
https://dictionary.cambridge.org/dictionary/english/fit-for-purpose.
[2] Computer Security Resource Center. *Fit for purpose: Definition.* National Institute of Standards and Technology. Retrieved December 29, 2025, from
https://csrc.nist.gov/glossary/term/Fit_for_purpose.

...created in Christ Jesus to do good works, which God prepared in advance for us to do. EPHESIANS 2:10 NIV

Consider a lock and key as an example of being fit for purpose.

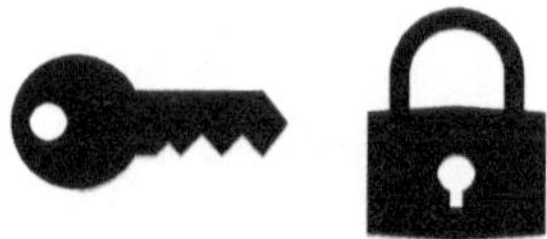

A key is designed for a specific purpose. Its size, shape, and structure are crafted to fit a particular lock. But being designed for the job isn't enough on its own. The key must be in the right place, at the right time, and in the right hand, ready and able to do its work in order to unlock the lock.

Now imagine that we are the key and our purpose is the lock. We must be fashioned in the right shape, be aligned, and be ready, willing, and available when the moment comes in order for us to accomplish our task. We can't be uncut, hanging out on the wrong key chain, or bent out of shape.

We all enter this world with a purpose for our life. Period. And just like the keys on this pegboard, we come in all different shapes, sizes, composition, and development.

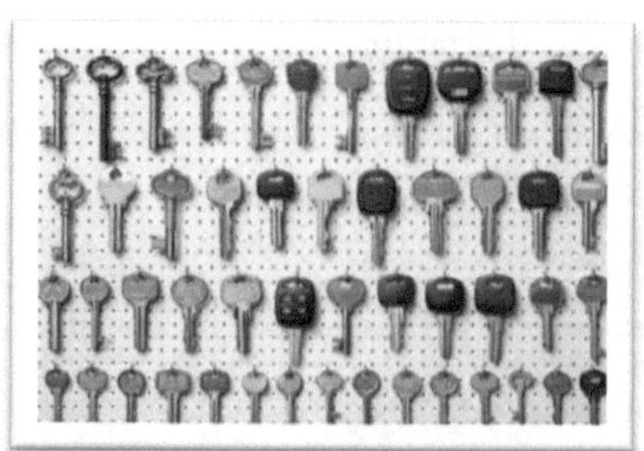

Image generated with OpenAI's DALL·E (January 2026).

We're all born with an inherent fitness: natural, God-given abilities and traits that give us a head start in life. But as we journey through life, we are continually shaped, stretched, and refined by the choices we make, the actions we take, and the circumstances we face. Some of these changes come from our own effort, like the hard work we put in to become stronger, wiser, and more capable. Other changes result from mistakes or poor decisions that cut deeper than we ever intended. And then there are the changes God brings, as He gently molds us with each turn of His potter's wheel. No matter the source, every shaping, every cut, and every refinement is for our good.

> *And we know that for those who love God all things work together for good, for those who are called according to his purpose.* ROMANS 8:28 ESV

The truth is, most people never fully step into their purpose; not because they weren't created for it, but because they aren't yet fit enough. To live fully and effectively, we must be whole, developing fitness across every area of life so we are ready to become the person we were meant to be.

Like a seed that refuses to crack open, untapped potential remains just that—potential. It only grows into what it was designed to be when we do the work to nurture it. And sometimes, that work feels like breaking or dying to what we were, so we can emerge as what we were meant to become.

GETTING FIT

Sometimes we need to get ourselves in shape through discipline, effort, and intentional action. Other times, we need to let God shape us and refine our hearts, realign our priorities, and prepare us for what we can't do on our own. Becoming fit for purpose requires both.

Getting Ourselves in Shape

Stepping into the purpose God has for us is not something that happens automatically. We have a responsibility to prepare ourselves for it. Just as an athlete trains or a musician practices, we must take intentional steps to become fit for the life and work God has designed for us. This requires honest self-reflection, taking ownership of our growth, and committing to deliberate action. Following are some steps to help you get started.

Take an Inventory

Before we can grow, we need to know where we actually stand. Taking an inventory means stepping back and looking honestly at every area of life including spiritual, emotional, physical, financial, relational, and vocational. Ask questions like: What's working well? What keeps breaking down? Where am I consistently stressed, stuck, or unprepared?

The hardest part about assessing our inventory is being honest about where we're weak. This isn't about shame; it's about clarity. Just like a doctor evaluates a patient before prescribing treatment, inventory gives direction, so our growth is intentional, not random. We can't grow what we refuse to acknowledge. That might mean facing habits, attitudes, wounds, or distractions that keep tripping us up.

It's tempting to hide our weak spots or excuse them, but unacknowledged weaknesses quietly control us. Being honest means admitting: "This is an area I struggle in, and it needs attention."

Weakness doesn't mean failure. It means we've found an area that needs strengthening, healing, or support. When we name it, we can pray about it, plan around it, and bring in the right tools or people to help.

Take Responsibility

Growth starts when we stop blaming circumstances, upbringing, or other people for everything that isn't working. Taking responsibility doesn't ignore any of the injustice or difficulty; it simply says, "What part of this can I influence or change?"

When we own our choices, our habits, and our responses, we reclaim authority over our lives. Responsibility moves us from victim mode to builder mode.

Take Action

Purpose never grows in hypotheticals. At some point, <u>we</u> have to move. Taking action means creating a plan, starting small, and staying consistent, even when it's uncomfortable.

That may look like:

- Signing up for counseling or coaching.
- Starting a savings plan.
- Setting a daily prayer or study routine.
- Practicing a new skill.
- Having hard but necessary conversations.

No action is still an action. If you're not doing it today, then you're not doing it. Once the plans are laid, any rumination over the plans for action is NOT action. Thinking about what you are going to do is not the same thing as doing it.

Intentions do NOT equal action. That's a hard truth to swallow. Stop putting off things for tomorrow. Even if you take only a small step today, no matter how minuscule it is, it's action AND progress.

Build Momentum

Each small step strengthens us for the next one, and over time, those steps lead us into someone who is truly fit for purpose.

The more you walk towards your purpose, the more rewarding it becomes, and the more steps you'll want to take.

Letting God Shape Us

WHY does God shape us?

In Scripture, God's glory is described as weighty, something that's substantial, powerful, and real. When His glory filled the temple, even trained priests couldn't stand under it. When His presence rested on the mountain, everything around it trembled. And Paul tells us that we are being prepared for an eternal weight of glory.

> *So we do not lose heart. Though our outer self is wasting away, our inner self is being renewed day by day. For this light momentary affliction is preparing for us an eternal weight of glory beyond all comparison,* 2 CORINTHIANS 4:16-17 ESV

This truth quietly answers a huge question about purpose: God doesn't just call us to do something. He prepares us to be someone like a challis that can carry what He gives.

Purpose isn't just about opportunity. It's about capacity.

If God's glory is weighty, then the purpose attached to that glory will also carry weight. This weight may look like responsibility, influence, leadership, impact, obedience, and faithfulness. And that means we have to grow strong enough (spiritually, emotionally, mentally, sometimes even physically) to handle it without collapsing under the pressure of it.

Just like a building must be reinforced before it can hold more weight, God strengthens and shapes us before He entrusts us with more of His work. That shaping may look like pruning, discipline, redirection, or seasons that stretch us, not because He's punishing us, but because He is fitting us to carry something precious.

Becoming fit for purpose requires our cooperation with the process of God as He tends to our character and deepens our roots. We must stay teachable and allow Him to build the resilience, strength, and faith we'll need to carry what He intends to place in our hands.

HOW does God shape us?

God rarely zaps us into readiness. Instead, He shapes us over time through growth, pressure, correction, opportunities, and grace. He works *in us* before He works *through us.*

- *He prunes us.* Pruning removes what looks alive but is actually stealing strength. God sometimes cuts back habits, relationships, attitudes, or commitments that keep us from bearing real fruit. It may feel like loss at first, but pruning creates space for deeper growth, clearer priorities, and more meaningful results.

- *He fertilizes us.* Fertilizer doesn't always come from pleasant places. Sometimes it's the BS we must endure. Nevertheless, fertilizer (no matter the kind) produces strong roots. God enriches us through teaching, experiences, mentors, trials, and blessings. These inputs nourish us so that when challenges come, we're grounded instead of shaken.

- *He presents kairos moments.* A kairos moment is a God-timed opportunity. It's not just *any* moment, but the *right* moment, and may come around only once in a lifetime. These are times when God opens doors or places us in the exact situation where obedience meets purpose. These moments require readiness and courage. They're invitations, not guarantees, so we must be vigilant to not miss them.

- *He delivers us.* Sometimes God just flat-out rescues us. He frees us from addictions, patterns, fears, and environments that hold us captive. These times in our life give birth to powerful testimonies that can set others free as well.

- *He uses people and circumstances.* God shapes us through community and real life. He sends mentors who teach, friends who support, critics who challenge, and situations that refine us. Even painful seasons can become classrooms, helping us grow compassion, wisdom, and humility. That person who is a real pain in your back side might be there to teach you something.

- *He encourages, warns, and provides knowledge.* The Holy Spirit is our internal trainer and guide. He comforts us when we're weary, convicts us when we're drifting, gives wisdom when we're unsure, and reminds us of truth when lies sound convincing. He shapes our inner life, so our outer life will align with God's purpose.

How we can recognize that God is "fitting" us?

Recognizing when God is actively shaping and fitting us for the purpose He has planned can be challenging. Often, His work is subtle, hidden in the rhythms of daily life, the challenges we face, and the lessons we're asked to learn. Yet, if we pay close attention, there are signs that reveal His hand at work, moments that stretch us, redirect us, and prepare us to step fully into the life He designed for us. By noticing these signals, we can respond appropriately, allowing His fitting to transform us from the inside out.

Following are some questions you can ask yourself to glean some insight.

Am I feeling uncomfortable? Growth feels uncomfortable. It just does. Anyone who has done a hard workout has experienced the uncomfortableness it produces in the body two days later. This is because exercise produces micro-tears in the muscles causing you to later experience the pain of inflammation, which triggers subsequent repair and growth of the muscle. You can't have muscle growth without this process.

You may have noticed seasons when God kept pressing on the same area, e.g., patience, pride, trust, forgiveness, or integrity. It's not random. It's like He's saying, "This part needs to be strengthened because it matters for where you're going."

God's fitting work often feels uncomfortable, but it produces growth.

Am I seeing patterns? God wired us to notice patterns. Have you ever researched a topic or had a conversation about something and then for the next several days, it seemed to pop up everywhere on TV, social media, overheard conversations, etc?

Pattern recognition is a tool God uses to get our attention. If you keep facing similar challenges, conversations, or lessons, that's often a sign God is teaching something that can't be skipped. He's drawing your attention to it. Once you respond differently (e.g., with wisdom instead of reaction) the pattern often shifts.

Is a door closing that I thought should have stayed open? Opportunities fade, relationships shift, and plans sometimes stall. It can feel unfair. Yet often, those closed doors are God's protection, steering us away from detours that could harm or distract us. Over time, we frequently realize that a "no" was making room for a far better "yes."

Do I feel stretched beyond my comfort zone? God often calls us into roles or moments that feel just a bit bigger than we are. Sometimes so big they seem downright impossible.

Those impossible moments feel that way for a reason. They aren't meant to be carried alone, and they reveal two important truths: either we lack an attribute or skill necessary for the task, or we are being invited to partner with God in such a way that His strength and power make the impossible possible.

Are new resources and/or voices suddenly appearing? Have you ever had a sermon suddenly speak exactly to a question you've been wrestling with? Or someone mentions a book or tool that opens your mind to a breakthrough you've been seeking? These are not coincidences. God knows exactly how and when to bring things or people into our lives for what lies ahead.

God often brings exactly what we need at exactly the right time. Sometimes it's a friend, a coworker, or a stranger who sparks a new idea, offers insight, or points us toward a solution we couldn't see on our own. Other times, it's an expert or resource that teaches us something essential for the next step in our journey.

Am I starting to see fruit in areas that once were weak? When God is "fitting" you, you'll often notice tangible, real-life fruit showing up in your thoughts and actions. Here are some examples:

- Greater patience in frustrating situations.
- Increased humility and teachability.
- A new job opening, promotion, or leadership role that aligns perfectly with your skills and calling.
- Acceptance into a program, school, or training.
- Unexpected financial blessing, gift, or windfall.
- Debt relief or new ways to manage resources.
- Reconciliation with someone after a long-standing conflict.

- Acquisition of a new skill or insight for something you've struggled with.
- A sense of purpose and alignment, even during challenges.

Old reactions will begin to change. You'll notice more peace, self-control, clarity, compassion, or wisdom. Growth becomes visible not because life got easier, but because you became stronger.

Sometimes we don't recognize God's working in our life until we reflect on it. Oftentimes, we can trace God's fingerprints in hindsight. Looking back, you may realize the previous season was hard, but it prepared you for the current one. Perspective can reveal that God wasn't punishing you. He was equipping you.

If you ever get to a place where you think God has overlooked you, then consider how many days on this earth He's allowed you another day to get it right. As I write this sentence, I'm reminded that for 19,311 days, God has kept me on this beautiful planet. Even if He's protected me only once a day, then I've been on His mind and heart 19,311 times. And friend, we both know He thinks about us more than once a day.

The following passage paints such a tender picture of God's innumerable thoughts toward us.

> *How precious to me are your thoughts, God! How vast is the sum of them! Were I to count them, they would outnumber the grains of sand—when I awake, I am still with you.* PSALM 139:17–18 NIV

How many times has God kept death from stealing you? Doesn't sound like you've been overlooked, does it?

How do we know whether it's God working in our life, or the enemy?

The truth is: it can be both.

Consider Job: God allowed the enemy to touch Job's life, not to destroy him, but for his ultimate growth and refinement. Through those trials, Job moved from *knowing about God* to truly *knowing God*. God did not cause the hardships, but He permitted them, using even the enemy's attacks to shape, strengthen, and prepare Job for a greater purpose.

The take-home message is: God uses everything for our betterment. Some things are directly from His hand, while others may come through the people in our life (either under God's influence or the enemy's).

> *And we know that in all things God works for the good of those who love him, who have been called according to his purpose.* ROMANS 8:28 NIV

Have you ever been stuck behind a slow driver when you were in a hurry? Or come down with a cold or the flu and had to miss something important?

I used to get incredibly frustrated when these sorts of things happened. Then one day, I had a striking realization. I was running late when a farm tractor pulled onto the narrow, two-lane country road ahead of me. We crawled along at about 20 mph for several miles. Eventually, I passed it, but not long after, I came upon a fatal accident. Had that tractor not slowed me down, I very well could have been the one in that crash. The timing was perfect for disaster. In that moment, I realized God had protected me.

Now, whenever I encounter delays or detours on the road (or in life), I pause and thank God. I recognize that these moments aren't just interruptions; they are part of His active work in shaping my life. Through these unexpected twists, He is guiding me, protecting me, and preparing me for what lies ahead, steering me toward the future He has planned.

With all this being said, we need to use discernment when we decide which things to tolerate in our life and which things to rebuke. Here are five red flags that may indicate the enemy is at work in our lives rather than God.

- *Persistent fear, anxiety, or discouragement.* When worry, doubt, or despair dominates your thoughts and prevents you from moving forward, it may be a spiritual attack rather than God's shaping work.
- *Confusion and deception.* If you're constantly misled, tempted to act against your values, or feel unable to discern truth from lies, the enemy may be trying to derail your path.
- *Isolation and broken relationships.* When relationships repeatedly break down or people around you are consistently drawn away, the enemy may be seeking to cut off your support and connection.
- *Repeated patterns of sin or destruction.* Struggling with the same destructive behaviors or cycles without seeing growth or correction can indicate the enemy exploiting vulnerabilities.
- *Loss of peace and godly perspective.* If your heart is continually restless, angry, or bitter, rather than calm, patient, and trusting in God, this may signal a spiritual attack rather than God's guiding hand.
- *Sense of condemnation.* Condemnation and conviction are different. Conviction comes from God, and its purpose is to point out what needs to change. It invites repentance, growth, and restoration. Even when it's uncomfortable, it

carries hope and a clear path forward. On the other hand, condemnation comes from the enemy. It brings feelings of shame and failure and paralyzes all hope. It offers no solution, only guilt, discouragement, and separation from God.

I have a friend who owns a multimillion-dollar company that experienced remarkable growth for more than a decade. From the outside, it looked strong, successful, and unstoppable. Then, without warning, a financial storm hit that threatened to wipe it out.

For an entire year, I watched my friend endure relentless pressure. What began as emotional strain soon manifested physically. It looked as though the enemy was cutting both him and his company to the bone, pushing them toward collapse. Yet day after day, he got up, faced one crisis after another, and clung to what often felt like a thinning thread of hope.

What no one realized at the time was that the daily crises were exposing something far more dangerous than the storm itself. Beneath the surface, the company was financially bleeding. Low employee utilization, inefficiencies, and structural weaknesses had been quietly draining its strength. Like a ship with hidden holes below the waterline, it was taking on water while the captain and crew believed everything was fine. Left unaddressed, the company was destined to sink.

Turns out, all the cuts and pain my friend endured during that year were not from the enemy's lashings, but from God's pruning shears.

God will lovingly but firmly prune the things in our lives that are dead, unproductive, or quietly sucking the life from us. Though pruning can feel painful and unsettling, it is necessary. When we endure this process, we emerge healthier, stronger, and capable of bearing lasting fruit that could not grow otherwise. But when pruning is avoided or resisted, the decay continues unseen, leaving us weakened and unprepared for the growth, responsibility, and calling God desires to entrust to us.

My friend endured the pruning, and the result was transformation. The company emerged healthier and stronger than ever, with a foundation solid enough to support growth that would have crushed its former version. What once looked like destruction was actually a rescue. What felt like an attack that would lead to death became the very process that saved the company and prepared it for lasting, sustainable growth.

God does this in our lives too. If we will let Him.

KNOW YOUR SEASON

Sometimes we need to find our "fit" in the season of life we're in.

Knowing what season of life you are in is crucial because each season comes with its own intent, challenges, and opportunities. Recognizing your current season helps you to respond appropriately.

Understanding your season also helps you prioritize your energy, make wise decisions, and align your actions with God's timing, ensuring that you're not wasting resources or resisting the very processes designed to forge a better you.

Not every season is the same, not all are pleasant, but each is necessary. God lets us know right up front that there is a time for everything.

> *A time to plant and a time to uproot,*
> *A time to kill and a time to heal,*
> *A time to tear down and a time to build,*
> *A time to weep and a time to laugh,*
> *A time to mourn and a time to dance,*

A time to scatter stones and a time to gather them,
A time to embrace and a time to refrain from embracing,
A time to search and a time to give up,
A time to keep and a time to throw away,
A time to tear and a time to mend,
A time to be silent and a time to speak,
A time to love and a time to hate,
A time for war and a time for peace.

ECCLESIASTES 3:2-8

As previously stated, purpose is not always one single "life assignment." It comes in layers. This is where seasons of life come into play.

Not every season is about leaving a lasting mark on the world. Only God can do that. Our work, even when it seems ordinary, has eternal significance.

The tasks we work on today may not be the same ones we find ourselves doing next year or twenty years from now. We are always growing, always being pruned, and like plants, our sprouts may reach in different directions depending on the position of the sun.

Sometimes our soil is fertile; sometimes we spend time in darkness before finding the light. Staying rooted is essential. Because we are made in the image of our Father, and He creates with His words, our own words have power to shape our environment over time.

The best response is to lean fully into the season we're in and make the most of the winds of change. Just as a kite cannot rise without leaning into the wind, we cannot ascend or grow unless we embrace the forces shaping us and allow them to lift us higher.

What are the general seasons in life?

Ages of Life

It's well known that each stage of life comes with its own experiences, responsibilities, and consequences.

The following are examples of age-related seasons that I totally made up. While these are not official by any capacity, they are useful for illustrating points and making general comparisons easier to understand.

- *1–18 years*: The learning and growing time. These are the foundational years of discovering the world and ourselves.
- *18–25 years*: The figuring out "Who am I?" and "What am I going to do with the rest of my life?" phase. This phase comes with pressure to make perfect, one-shot decisions. It may feel like this first try at adulting will set the course for everything.
- *25–50 years*: The adulting in full swing time. Here we live out the decisions made in the previous season, build a career, raise a family, and learn the realities of parenting.
- *50–75 years*: This season often begins with an empty nest and a lost sense of self. We may feel tired of the routine and ready for something new. But we ask ourselves where to start when we're already this old. This season is, however, completely full of fresh opportunities.
- *75+ years*: Retirement years (I haven't been here yet, so I can only imagine!) This stage often involves teaching, mentoring, and sharing wisdom across generations, as well as using our life experiences as tools to guide, inspire, and shape others.

It is of utmost importance to NOT define your season by age alone.

When I was a kid, 50-year-olds seemed like crypt-keepers. They had white hair, frumpy clothes, and a certain "old-person" vibe. Contrast that with today's vibrant, confident, and stylish 50-year-olds, especially women. You see it even in Hollywood: some of the most sought-after and highest-paid actors and actresses are 45 and older, still rivaling younger stars in beauty, energy, and presence. In today's world, people are living longer, healthier lives well into their 70s and 80s, and reaching 95 is increasingly achievable and becoming more common.

New trends and common practices like hormone replacement therapy, preventive medicine and early detection, and advanced recovery technologies are helping people stay younger, stronger, and sharper than previous generations.

As we age, our perception of time changes, often creating false limitations. Think about everything that happens between 25 and 50 years of age: raising children, building a career, pursuing education, and so much more. The same possibilities exist for those who are 50 and beyond. There's no real difference—only the excuses we tell ourselves. A 50-year-old can experience just as much growth, adventure, and opportunity from 50 to 75 as they did in the earlier decades of life. And likewise for 75 and beyond. Twenty years is another life of opportunity that is achievable for those even in their 70s.

Existential crises used to be thought of as a hallmark of midlife, a period when people paused to question their purpose, accomplishments, and legacy. Today, however, the landscape has shifted. With the constant pressures of social media, online comparison, cyberbullying, 24/7 connectivity, economic uncertainty, and the endless stream of information at our fingertips, even younger people can experience these deep questions about meaning and direction. The speed of modern life, the expectation to "have it all figured out," and the constant visibility of others' successes can bring feelings of inadequacy, doubt, and anxiety much earlier, forcing many to confront existential questions decades sooner than previous generations.

It's easy to let time and age feel like a barrier, but more often than not, the real barrier is our mindset. Age doesn't limit what's possible; it simply challenges us to lean in, adapt, and embrace the opportunities before us.

Our Past

Current scientific principles affirm a simple truth: what's done is done. The past is forever out of our reach.

Scripture has said the same thing for centuries. *"for behold, the winter is past; the rain is over and gone."*[3] We are repeatedly instructed not to dwell on what has already passed. *"Forget the former things; do not dwell on the past."*[4]

The only way the past becomes alive again is if we carry it into the present.

Think about a mirror. When you look into one, you are always seeing an older version of yourself (even if only by milliseconds). Fixating on the mirror instead of moving forward distorts how you live now. In the same way, living in the past warps the present and obstructs the future.

---

[3] Song of Solomon 2:11 ESV
[4] Isaiah 43:18 NIV

I recently saw a social media post (author unknown) that captured this beautifully:

Forgive yourself for not knowing earlier what only time could teach.

Modern neuroscience reinforces this wisdom. Medical researchers have discovered that the same regions of the brain used to recall the past are also used to imagine and plan the future.[5] This explains why individuals with severe memory loss struggle to envision tomorrow, and why the same impairment appears in people suffering from suicidal depression.

In simple terms, when your brain is occupied in reliving the past, it cannot be used to visualize the future. Researchers are only now articulating what Christians have understood for thousands of years.

Christians recognize that we have an adversary, the accuser of the brethren. He continually reminds us of our failures, mistakes, and regrets. Why? Because he knows that a person trapped in the past becomes ineffective in the future. He understands this "brain game."

To overcome our enemy, we must do exactly what Scripture commands: do not dwell on the past. We must bury yesterday's failures and redirect our focus toward envisioning how we can be more effective for the Kingdom tomorrow.

Simply put, we must learn to see past our past.

When we ruminate, past events become present realities. What belongs to yesterday should stay there; it should not define today.

---

[5] Szpunar KK, Watson JM, McDermott KB. Neural substrates of envisioning the future. Proc Natl Acad Sci USA. 2007;104(2):642-647.

If you are reading this now, you have survived everything the enemy has thrown at you with a 100% success rate. You are an overcomer. Know it. Act like it.

Today

It's ALWAYS today. It's NEVER yesterday or tomorrow. Now can only be now. Yes, this seems simple, and yet it's so profound.

But what does this really mean?

The person we are right now should never look like the person from our past or our future. We continuously evolve. It's impossible to remain the same. Either we are growing better or growing worse. Either in the right direction, or the wrong. All by our choice.

So, what should we be doing *today*?

Scripture repeatedly anchors God's people in the urgency and responsibility of today.

God again set a certain day, calling it "Today" HEBREWS 4:7 NIV

Today is not incidental. It is *the* divinely appointed space where obedience, faith, and perseverance are exercised.

Jesus reinforces this present-moment focus by warning us not to live in anxiety about the future.[6] The future is uncertain by design, and we do not know what a day may bring.[7] Because tomorrow is unknowable, God calls us to faithful action now.

This principle of *today* was woven into Israel's daily life. The Israelites didn't worry about providing for the Sabbath because

---

[6] Matthew 6:34
[7] Proverbs 27:1

God supplied what they needed the day before. Their responsibility was obedience today, trusting God for provision beyond it. Likewise, God places choices before us in the present moment, and the decision is not postponed—it is always made today.

> *See, I set before you today life and prosperity, death and destruction*
> DEUTERONOMY 30:15 NIV

While Scripture promises a future rest, it also makes clear that this is not the season for spiritual inactivity.[8] We are not called to rest now, because there is Kingdom work to be done.

Our posture, then, is to remain fully engaged in today. We labor on earth in alignment with heaven, praying as Jesus taught us: May your will be done on earth as it is in heaven.[9]

Today is where God's will is carried out, His Kingdom advanced, and our faith proven. All of this is accomplished, not in yesterday or tomorrow, but by how we live, obey, and choose today.

How can you identify your specific season?

We move through far more seasons in life than we realize. Consider a tree: it must reinvent itself four times every year (spring, summer, fall, winter) without complaint or choice. Many trees live 100 to 300 years, which means they endure roughly 400 to 1,200 distinct seasons over a single lifetime.

Humans experience seasons differently, but no less frequently. The average person now holds about fifteen different jobs over a

---

[8] Hebrews 4:9-11
[9] Matthew 6:10

career. Each decade of life tends to bring its own distinct season, i.e., childhood, young adulthood, midlife, later life. Add to that the major life events that reshape us: deaths, weddings, births, illnesses. Then layer in all the miscellaneous transitions such as moves, callings, awakenings, losses, restorations. Even if none of these ever overlapped (which they absolutely do), you are easily looking at fifty meaningful seasons in one life. And unlike the tree, which never asks itself whether it's tired of being a tree, we are conscious participants. We have agency, awareness, and responsibility in how we respond to each season we're given.

What complicates things further is that we are rarely in just one season at a time. You might be in a season of professional growth while simultaneously walking through grief in your personal life. Your body may be in a rebuilding season while your faith feels dormant. Or vice versa. A marriage can be flourishing while finances are under strain. Just because one area of your life is in winter does not mean everything else is. Life is layered, and our seasons often overlap, intersect, and even conflict with one another.

Because fitness is the unifying theme of this book, we'll use sports seasons as our working analogy: draft, off-season, training, competition, recovery, and rebuilding. What follows are clear descriptions of each of these seasons, how to recognize them, and what they tend to look like when you're living through them.

Draft Season

Draft season is all about standing at a crossroads of decision. It's the pause before movement, the inhale before commitment. Nothing is finalized yet, but everything feels possible. And weighty.

This season is defined by waiting, evaluating, and then choosing. It's transitional by nature, asking you to look honestly at where you've been, discern where you're being pulled next, and accept that whatever comes after will be shaped by the decisions you make here.

We all recognize certain draft seasons because they arrive with cultural mile markers. High school graduation brings the first major one: college, trade school, military, work. Each path carries consequences and opportunities. Embarking on parenting marks another profound transition, where your identity expands and your priorities reorder themselves. Choosing a first career or job is another defining crossroads, often made with limited information but enormous hope. These moments feel monumental because they are, and yet they are also just the first of many.

What surprises most people is that crossroads are not one-and-done events. We often find ourselves standing in familiar places again, only with more experience and more at stake. Revisiting a crossroads doesn't mean you failed the first time; it often means you've grown enough to see new options that weren't visible before.

One of the most common repeated crossroads is career choice, especially in midlife. If this is you, know this: what you're facing now is remarkably similar to the decisions you made after high school or college. Look at the lifetime you've already lived since then, including education, career, family, mistakes, wins, resilience. Now realize this: you have the opportunity for that same amount of life and time still ahead of you. You can choose a new career, go back to school, pursue a long-suppressed passion, or take a next step shaped by wisdom instead of guesswork. This season invites you to redefine what "success" looks like now. Find the intersection of your experience, skills, and passion, and pursue it with intention.

If you find yourself standing at a career crossroads again, ask yourself a simple question: What suggestions would I give a brand-new high school graduate standing here? Then take your own advice. Treat your midlife decision with the same hope, seriousness, and openness you would encourage in someone just starting out, trusting that God had not run out of purpose simply because time had passed.

Choosing the right path is monumentally important. Scripture speaks often and seriously about paths. The book of Proverbs warns of those who leave the straight paths to walk in dark ways.[10] The psalmist prays: "Show me your ways, Lord, and teach me your paths,"[11] recognizing that right paths are learned, not assumed. Jeremiah warns against forgotten and broken paths and urges that the soil of the heart to be broken up before new growth begins.[12] Choosing a path is not neutral—it is formative.

Here's the good news: you don't have to choose the *perfect* path because there isn't one. Don't burden yourself with the pressure of picking the flawless major, career, or life plan. You will change jobs. Your interests will evolve. Life will turn in unexpected ways. That doesn't mean you chose wrong; it means you're alive and growing.

If you struggle to discern the next step, bow humbly in prayer. When humility meets obedience, your nose will eventually hit the

---

10 Proverbs 2:13
11 Psalm 25:4
12 Jeremiah 18:15 and 4:3

path beneath your feet. As Peter reminds us, to make every effort to confirm your calling and election so that we will never stumble.[13]

Don't camp at the crossroads either. One danger of draft season is lingering too long. *Next year will come whether you make an effort or not.* And if you make no changes today, you'll arrive there unchanged and carrying regret for the time and opportunity lost. Think about physical fitness: you can't reach your ideal body in two weeks, but you can absolutely find it in a year. That year is coming whether you act or not. So, why not be who you want to be when it arrives?

Small changes, sustained over time, are far easier and far more effective than massive, immediate overhauls. Goals that are too big or too fast become smothering and restrictive, breeding bitterness and resentment. No one likes to be controlled. But, everyone likes to be in control. Choose small changes you can govern, rather than big ones that govern you.

Another warning Scripture offers is not to follow paths that aren't yours. Proverbs cautions that some paths lead to death, and that others may entice you toward a way that is not good.[14] Comparison, pressure, and persuasion can pull you off course if you're not paying attention. Your path may not look impressive to others, but it must be faithful, life-giving, and aligned with truth.

Finally, make it a habit to conduct an annual check-up. Ask yourself honestly: Am I in a different place than I was last year? If the answer is no, stagnation has set in. Growth doesn't require dramatic change. It does require, however, movement. Even small

---

[13] 2 Peter 1:10
[14] Proverbs 2:18 and 16:29

forward steps, taken consistently, prove that you're still on the path and not stuck standing at the crossroads.

Training Season

Training season is the space between calling and capacity. It's the intentional period where strength is built, skills are sharpened, and weaknesses are exposed. This season isn't flashy and it rarely feels urgent, yet it is essential. Training season exists to close the gap between where you are now and what the next season of purpose will require of you.

Before God advances us, He often equips us. That training may be practical such as education, certifications, leadership skills, financial stewardship, communication, or discipline. It may also be internal and address patience, humility, emotional regulation, obedience, endurance, or trust. Sometimes the training is spiritual, teaching us to hear God's voice more clearly, deepen our prayer life, or developing discernment. At times, we must undergo physical training to strengthen our bodies so we can endure or perform what the next season will demand. For example, you can't hike among mountain villages to do missionary work if you can't even catch your breath on the stairs.

You can often tell you're in a training season scheduled by God when progress feels slow but intentional. Doors may feel closed, yet preparation opportunities keep appearing. You may sense God saying, "not yet," while repeatedly placing tools, mentors, or stretching assignments in your path. Another sign is repetition. You may be asked to practice the same lesson over and over until it becomes instinct. If the calling feels clear but the timing doesn't, training season is likely already on the calendar.

Some training seasons are short, intense, and uncomfortable. High-intensity training compresses growth into a brief window through pressure, challenge, or crisis. You're forced to adapt quickly, learn fast, and shed inefficiencies. Spiritually, this may look like accelerated learning, rapid pruning, or being placed in situations that demand immediate obedience and resilience. These seasons are exhausting, but they produce sharp clarity and rapid maturity.

Other seasons focus less on intensity and more on staying power. Endurance training is about consistency over time by showing up again and again, without immediate reward. In life, this looks like faithfulness in unseen work, perseverance through long delays, or steady obedience when emotions fluctuate. God often uses endurance training to prepare us for responsibilities that require longevity rather than speed.

At times, training season is about adding mass, also known as bulking. This might involve acquiring knowledge, building networks, expanding influence, or increasing confidence. At other times, it's about cutting, letting go of excess weight that slows you down. God may strip away distractions, unhealthy relationships, misplaced ambition, or self-reliance. Both are forms of training. One adds capacity, while the other increases efficiency.

Not all training is about strength or endurance. Some seasons are about precision. Skill refinement focuses on doing fewer things better and may address sharpening your craft, improving judgment, or learning when not to act. Mobility training, on the other hand, restores range of motion. In life, this may look like healing from past wounds, relearning trust, or gaining flexibility in thinking and responding. Strength without mobility leads to injury. Purpose without healing leads to burnout.

No matter what type of training season you are in, get fully engaged. Training season requires participation. Sometimes that means actively enrolling, practicing, studying, and stretching yourself on purpose. Other times, it means surrender (i.e., submitting to the process God is designing, even when you wouldn't choose the workout yourself). Whether you're picking up the weights or being handed them, the goal is the same: readiness. Training season is not punishment—it's preparation.

Performance Season

Performance season (sometimes called competition season) is the time when preparation turns into execution. This is when you step onto the field, into the arena, or onto the course and do the work you've been training for. It's not about getting ready anymore; it's about showing up and applying what you've built. Performance season is active and demanding. It's where purpose moves from potential to practice.

For some, performance season looks like projects launching and responsibilities stacking. You may feel stretched but capable, tired but focused. There's momentum here, a sense that what you're doing matters now. Feedback is more immediate, stakes feel higher, and effort has real-world consequences. This season often requires sharper boundaries, clearer priorities, and the discipline to say no to anything that dilutes your focus.

At the same time, performance season doesn't always feel heroic. Some days it's repetitive, unglamorous, and quiet. Faithfulness may look like doing the same right thing again—making the call, showing up, finishing the task—without applause. Progress is real, but it may be measured in inches rather than miles.

Not all performance seasons move at the same pace. Sometimes it's a sprint and other times it's a marathon. And sometimes it's more like an obstacle race: you run hard for a while, then slam into an obstacle, climb, crawl, or carry weight, and then get back to running again. Purpose often unfolds this way with bursts of progress followed by challenges that force you to slow down, adapt, and dig deeper before moving forward.

Performance season can be brutal at times. I've learned this firsthand running Spartan races, which are long-distance obstacle course races that combine trail running with physically demanding challenges like climbing ropes, carrying heavy loads, crawling through mud, and scaling walls. There are moments when your lungs burn, your legs are shot, and you're questioning why you signed up in the first place. You'll have strong moments and weak ones. You'll see people pass you (sometimes easily). You may even face setbacks that force you to repeat obstacles or adjust your pace. What I learned is this: difficulty doesn't mean you're failing. It means you're doing something that requires effort. The course doesn't get easier. Definitely not. But you get tougher by staying in it.

When we talk about competition in the context of purpose, it's important to be clear: you are not competing against other people. Comparison is one of the fastest ways to drain joy from performance season. I'm proud to say I have four Spartan Trifectas under my belt. A trifecta means completing three different Spartan races (5k Sprint, 10k Super, and a 21k Beast) within the same year. To some readers, that may sound impressive, and to others, it may sound small. Just know that there are athletes out there who complete a trifecta every month and have done so for several years. And that's the point. We must run our own race, not someone else's. There will always be someone stronger, faster, or more accomplished. You just haven't met them yet, and it's possible they may still be in diapers.

The real competition is against distraction, fatigue, complacency, and the temptation to quit early. You are competing against the version of yourself that would rather stay comfortable than faithful. Performance season isn't about beating others. It's about finishing what you were called to run.

Even in performance season, rest is not a failure. It's sometimes a requirement. Just like in a marathon, you still need to refuel and rehydrate. You may even need to walk for a stretch instead of running. That doesn't disqualify you; it keeps you going. Ignoring your limits leads to injury, burnout, or collapse before the finish line. Sustainable performance honors the body, the mind, and the soul. Sometimes the most strategic move in performance season is slowing down just enough to finish strong.

Losing Season

A losing season is a time when progress feels stalled, momentum seems lost, or life seems to push back against your efforts. Unlike a season of rest, which is intentional and restorative, a losing season is often unexpected and uncomfortable. Rest comes with purpose and renewal, while losing seasons feel like resistance, setbacks, or obstacles that slow you down despite your best efforts. In a losing season, the world doesn't pause and instead, it pushes, and you feel like you're barely keeping up.

Though painful, losing seasons are essential for growth. They stretch our character, clarify our priorities, and prepare us for what's ahead. Consider the arrow: it only flies forward after being pulled backward. Losing seasons function like that pull. Without the tension, without the apparent setback, we can't build the force or momentum needed to move forward. They shape resilience, refine focus, and sometimes redirect us toward the trajectory God intends.

During a losing season, life can feel heavy, discouraging, or confusing. Plans fall through, efforts don't yield expected results, and frustration or doubt can creep in. You may feel stuck in routines that no longer serve you, or face challenges that test patience and perseverance. It's a season where you sense the friction between where you are and where you want to be, and the gap can feel discouraging or even defeating.

Some people find themselves asking whether God still uses people who have failed before. And the resounding answer is YES! God can absolutely still use us, even if we've failed before. In fact, Scripture shows again and again that God often works through failure, not around it. Failure doesn't disqualify you; unrepentance and unwillingness do. God is a redeemer by nature. He takes what is broken, wasted, or misused and weaves it into something purposeful. Our past mistakes don't surprise Him or limit Him. When we surrender them, they become part of our testimony, giving us humility, compassion, and credibility we wouldn't have gained any other way. God isn't looking for perfect people. He's looking for willing ones. If you're still breathing, He's not finished.

Not every difficult season is a losing season, but some seasons mimic that losing feeling closely. The next sections will explore these specific experiences: the Ecclesiastes season, where meaning and motivation seem absent; the winter season, marked by stillness, waiting, and apparent dormancy; and the dark night of the soul, a deeply spiritual season of testing and inner struggle. Understanding these seasons helps us distinguish temporary setbacks from purposeful preparation.

Ecclesiastes Season

One particular kind of difficult season is what I call an Ecclesiastes season, named after Solomon's reflections on life. This is not a season of obvious loss or outward failure, but of internal reckoning. It's the moment when you pause, look around at everything you've done, and quietly ask, "What was all of this for?"

Solomon had everything (wisdom, wealth, influence, achievement), and yet Ecclesiastes reads like the journal of someone who has reached the summit only to find the view strangely empty. This season feels marked by apathy. Nothing excites you the way it once did. You've "been there, done that," and it doesn't feel worth repeating. Commitments feel heavy. Obligations feel intrusive. You don't want to be tied down because life suddenly feels too short to waste on anything that doesn't feel deeply meaningful. Long-term desires fade. Big dreams and lofty aspirations lose their pull. You're not chasing anymore; you're questioning why you ever chased at all.

An Ecclesiastes season is not the same as depression, though the two can coexist. This season is not marked by sadness, despair, or hopelessness. You can still enjoy life. You still laugh, sleep, and function. There isn't necessarily fatigue, anxiety, or a loss of pleasure. Instead, the dominant question is quieter and more unsettling: "What now?" It's an existential pause, not an emotional collapse.

I entered my own Ecclesiastes season a few months after my dad died. One day, I drove past his house, the place where so much life had happened. That house held countless memories, especially the hours he spent playing and singing the songs he wrote. He was a self-taught musical genius who would serenade me for hours, making me feel like the most important person in the world. He was endlessly creative and built gadgets, designed unique landscapes, and invented beauty out of nothing. But when I drove by that day, the house was gone. The new owner had bulldozed it into its basement and covered it with dirt. All that remained was bare earth. In that moment, it hit me hard: all that life, all that joy, all that creativity now lived only in the memories in my head. And when I die, it will be gone forever.

No one passing by would ever know the melodies that filled that space or the stories that unfolded there. My dad's entire life of creativity seemed to have vanished without a trace. And suddenly, I wasn't just grieving the loss of my father. I was questioning my own life. Was I where I was supposed to be? Had everything I'd done meant anything at all? Did I have enough life left to make up for what I missed?

This is the heart of an Ecclesiastes season. You look back and wonder if an entire season, or even your whole life, was a failure. You may begin to wonder if you heard God wrong, chose the wrong path, or misunderstood your calling altogether. That doubt is dangerous. It can paralyze you, convincing you that you can't hear God clearly and therefore shouldn't move forward at all. And this is where the enemy often steps in, not with loud accusations, but with quiet reinforcement and whispers of how you should stop trying, stop believing, and stop hoping that anything you do will truly matter.

If you find yourself in an Ecclesiastes season, take intentional steps to move through it rather than get stuck in it. Solomon ultimately decided that the answer lies in fearing God and keeping His commandments, finding meaning in faithful obedience even when life feels fleeting or empty. One practical step is to seek out someone who has walked through a similar season and emerged on the other side. Their perspective and encouragement can help illuminate the path forward. If you cannot yet find your own sense of purpose, trust God's promises that He works in all things for the good of those who love him.[15] Remember, not every success or life contribution is immediately visible. Some seeds take years or even generations to bear fruit. My father's life, for example, continues to live on as I share his story with others, including my children, their children, and even you. The impact of a life well lived may not be erased, even when it seems buried. It can echo far beyond the present moment, reminding us that purpose and legacy often unfold over time.

---

[15] Romans 8:28

If you feel like your remaining days aren't enough, don't lose hope. God can transform a moment, a minute, or an hour in ways that defy human logic. In one minute from now, your life could be radically different. Scripture is full of stories showing that God can do more in an instant than we could accomplish in a lifetime: where God added years to Hezekiah's life; where God caused the sun to stand still so Joshua could secure victory; where God delivered Peter from prison in response to the prayers of the disciples; and where God instantly transported Ezekiel to see visions and fulfill His calling. [16] These accounts remind us that no amount of time is too short for God's intervention.

I've seen God intervene in the passage of time in my own life in ways that left me astonished. There was the time while driving to my dad's court hearing. A trip that normally took several hours was completed in a fraction of the expected time, without ever exceeding the speed limit, and witnessed by my friend riding with me. And once, when trying to get my daughter to a worship service on time, a journey that should have taken a set number of minutes somehow took far less, again without speeding. Each experience reminded me that God is not constrained by clocks or calendars. His timing can stretch or compress reality so that what seems impossible becomes possible.

Winter Season

People love winter for its quiet beauty of snow-softened landscapes, its crisp, refreshing air, and its enticement to slow down. But the other face of old man winter can be harsh and

---

[16] 2 Kings 20:1-11, Joshua 10:1-14, Acts 12:1-19, Ezekiel 8:2-4

unforgiving. Similarly, a winter season in life often feels cold, lonely, stripped of visible growth, and barren. Unlike a true losing season, which may feel like external setbacks or resistance, or an Ecclesiastes season, which carries questioning, doubt, and disillusionment, winter feels still and dormant. Yet, this stillness is not emptiness. It's a preparatory pause, a season designed for rest, reflection, and hidden growth beneath the surface.

Winter seasons serve a vital purpose: they create the conditions for new life to emerge. Just as seeds appear lifeless in the cold soil, so too must certain aspects of our lives undergo a kind of death before growth can occur. The chill and stillness of winter allow roots to deepen, systems to strengthen, and preparation to happen in unseen ways. If this process doesn't take place, the seeds cannot sprout. What looks dead on the surface is often alive and growing underneath, building the foundation for future seasons of abundance and vitality.

If anything understands the winter season, it's winter wheat. Winter wheat is a type of wheat that is planted in the fall and produces a harvest in the following summer. It requires a period of cold, called vernalization, to trigger proper development. Winter wheat is typically hardier, yielding more than spring wheat.

The first great act of winter wheat is obedient surrender to the process. Buried in darkness, it takes on water, swells, and then splits open; the seed, as it was, ceases to exist. To an outside eye, this looks like death: the dissolving of form, the loss of identity, the quiet undoing of what once was whole. And yet, this "death" is precisely what makes life possible. The seed does not experience progress as triumph, but as breaking. If it feels anything, it would not be the joy of becoming wheat, but the ache of undoing, an ending that feels final. Only later, unseen and unannounced, does life emerge from what was lost, proving that in winter wheat, as in so much of life, growth often arrives disguised as extinction.

When you find yourself in a winter season that feels lifeless, remember that God may be working on seeds already planted in your life. This is the time to dig deep and draw strength from your roots of faith, experiences, and wisdom.

Life continues to grow even where we cannot see it, under the surface, in quiet preparation. Do not lose hope. Winter is not the end or death. It is actually the beginning of new things. Every morning emerges from the night, and every spring forward follows a winter of preparation. Trust that God's work in this season is unseen but intentional and watch for your new purpose to break forth.

Dark Night of the Soul

A dark night of the soul is an intense, deeply spiritual, and profoundly existential season where life feels heavy, confusing, and stripped of clarity. It is painful and disorienting, often provoking not only questions of faith, but of meaning, identity, and purpose. During this time, you may feel isolated, uncertain, and spiritually dry. Daily routines can feel hollow, prayer may seem distant, and joy may appear unreachable. This is a refining fire that strips you from reliance on comfort, certainty, and control, leaving you exposed and ready for transformation.

If you find yourself in this kind of season, it is crucial to lean into God even if His presence feels distant. Trust Him through this deep trial and stay in prayer, even when words fail. Remember that God is improving, not abandoning, you. Although fires are hot and painful, they purify what is precious and remove what can no longer be endured.

Do not withdraw and isolate yourself during a dark night of the soul! It is critical to find someone trained and trustworthy to talk to. Find a counselor, pastor, therapist, or spiritual director who can help you navigate what you're experiencing. This season can leave you emotionally and spiritually exposed, and unwelcome or intrusive thoughts, including suicidal thoughts, can sometimes penetrate the mind during this time. If that happens, it is not a failure of faith; it is a signal that you need support. Do not try to endure this season alone. God often brings healing and clarity through the presence and care of others, and reaching out is an act of wisdom and courage. Help is part of the provision God makes for survival and restoration in the darkest seasons.

These seasons are not meaningless suffering. They are opportunities for profound spiritual growth and realignment with His purposes. Endurance, patience, and faith during the dark night prepare you to step into a season of clarity, strength, and renewed purpose.

Due Season

My greatest lesson about due season came from a surprising place—from the wisdom of a young child. Scripture tells us that children often perceive what adults overlook.[17]

---

[17] Matthew 11:25

Kids carry a depth of wisdom unencumbered by cynicism and the need to control outcomes. They see truth simply, intuitively, and without all the mental noise adults accumulate. My daughter Julia taught me about due season when she was just eight years old, opening my eyes to something I had read countless times but never truly seen.

Julia has always been deeply artistic, showing creative expression from a very young age. During church services while listening to the sermon, she would quietly occupy her hands by drawing, writing, and creating. (Yes, parents… they *are* listening, even when they look busy doing other things.)

One Sunday morning, she wrote and illustrated a short story during the service. It was about a lonely sunflower who found joy through her tears, inspired by the verse: *"Those who sow with tears will reap with songs of joy."*[18]

In the story, a lonely sunflower cried and cried and cried, so much so, that her tears watered the ground around her. In time, other flowers began to grow, and in the end, the sunflower and her new friends all sang a song of joy together. It was tender, hopeful, and remarkably insightful. At its core, Julia's little book carried a profound truth: we reap what we sow. It was the very principle of due season, told with childlike clarity and faith.

That story eventually became more than a moment. It became a book. Award-winning artist Kasey Short took Julia's original drawings and transformed them into beautiful, professional illustrations while preserving the heart and innocence of Julia's

---

[18] Psalm 126:5 NIV

vision. What began as a quiet act of listening and creating during church became a published reminder that God often speaks through the smallest voices to convey the biggest truths.

This is me as a parent shamelessly bragging about my baby:

The lessons of sowing and reaping are woven throughout Scripture, and God is clear about the promise of due season.

Let us not grow weary of doing good, for in due season we shall reap, if we do not give up GALATIANS 6:9 ESV

Yet so often, we want to decide the timing ourselves. We assume we know when the harvest should come, and when it doesn't arrive on our schedule, we lose hope and conclude that God has said "no"; when in reality, He is simply saying, "not yet."

God's "not yet" is not the same as "no." Read that again.

Delay is not denial, and waiting is often part of God's design. Every seed has its season. Every promise has its time. You <u>will</u> reap in due season. So, the question becomes: what are you sowing right now?

Out of Season

Being out of season is not the same as resting or recovering. It is a condition of misalignment when capacity, readiness, or fruitfulness does not match the moment that demands it. To be out of season is to lack what is required when the opportunity arrives. It's not about timing alone; it's about preparedness.

In everyday terms, being out of season shows up clearly. Physically, it looks like being out of shape when strength or endurance is required. Financially, it may mean living without margin when a crisis hits. Professionally, it can look like being unskilled or undisciplined when advancement is offered. Spiritually, it often presents as apathy, passivity, or indifference. People who are out of season may appear distracted, unmotivated, disengaged, or full of good intentions that never materialize into action.

Scripture gives sobering examples of the danger of appearing ready without actually being prepared. One of the clearest is the fig tree Jesus cursed. Though it was not fig season, the tree was in leaf thus signaling potential fruit. When Jesus found none, He cursed it, and it withered. This wasn't about agricultural timing; it was about spiritual readiness. The fig tree symbolized outward appearance without inward fruitfulness. Leaves without fruit. Promise without substance. Jesus used this moment to teach that faith, obedience, and readiness matter, whereas image does not.

Another striking example appears in the parable of the ten virgins. All ten looked prepared. All were invited. But only five had oil when the moment arrived. The others were spiritually out of season, unready when readiness mattered most. Opportunity does not wait for preparation to catch up.

Scripture repeatedly urges us to live in a state of readiness. Paul echoes this urgency when he tells us to not be like others, who are asleep, but be awake and sober.[19] Readiness is not episodic. It's a posture.

One of the clearest expressions of readiness is our testimony. Being prepared to give an answer isn't just about having the right words. It's about living in alignment with God so that hope is evident when questions come.

> ...*Always be prepared to give an answer to everyone who asks you to give the reason for the hope that you have* 1 PETER 3:15 NIV

Notice the word *always*. Not when it's comfortable. Not when it's convenient. Not when you feel inspired. Always.

Apathy isn't the only signpost of being out of season; empty intentions are another. It's not enough to mentally catalog everything you plan to do someday. Intentions without follow-through produce no fruit. Being out of season often sounds productive but remains inactive. Fruit requires action.

Bear in mind that being burned out is not the same as being out of season. Burnout signals the need for recovery, restoration, and rehab; all necessary down times that serve a purpose and are addressed later in *Be Okay With Down Times*. But being lukewarm? That IS out of season. Indifference, disengagement, and spiritual neutrality are <u>not</u> acceptable states. While seasons of rest and

---

[19] 1 Thessalonians 5:6

recovery are necessary, seasons of apathy are not. Being out of season is less about weakness and more about unwillingness. And Scripture makes clear that readiness is not optional.

PINPOINT YOUR TRAINING GROUND

We need to find the place where progress begins. The hardest part of beginning something new is knowing where or how to even start. That question feels difficult because starting can feel overwhelming when the destination seems far away. Our minds jump ahead to the outcome, the effort required, and the uncertainty along the way. The weight of the end goal can eclipse the simplicity of the first step. Instead of identifying the initial training ground, we overthink the entire journey. Yet God rarely reveals the full map. More often, He reveals only the next place of obedience, asking us to trust Him one step at a time.

This question of knowing where to begin matters because progress requires the right environment. Growth doesn't happen by accident; it happens in settings designed to produce it. Just as a boxer wouldn't prepare for a fight in a library, purpose-driven growth requires a space aligned with the outcome we seek. The environment we choose either accelerates progress or quietly works against it. Without the right training ground, even the best intentions struggle to gain traction.

To identify the right training ground, we must ask honest questions. Where am I resisting structure? Where is God asking for consistency? What environment would stretch me instead of soothe me? These questions expose whether we are seeking comfort or growth, and whether we are willing to submit to a process instead of chasing a quick result.

Once the need is clear, the training ground must match it. If you want to improve your physical health, you join a gym or commit to a structured fitness plan. If you need a new skill or credential, you enroll in a course, pursue a certification, or return to school. If your finances need strengthening, you may need budgeting tools, financial coaching, or accountability. If your leadership needs sharpening, you step into responsibility rather than avoiding it. Each outcome has a corresponding place of training.

When we think of training grounds, we often picture gyms or classrooms, but many are not physical locations at all. Emotional growth may take place in honest conversations instead of avoidance, or in group therapy rather than isolation. Character development often occurs when we accept a leadership assignment that stretches us beyond our comfort zone. Preparation for future provision may happen through education, certifications, apprenticeships, or seasons of disciplined learning that feel slow but are deeply formative.

Training grounds are often ordinary, but not obvious. We tend to expect dramatic shifts or sudden breakthroughs, but God frequently uses practical, accessible environments to shape us. The training ground is usually closer than we think, but it may require humility to enter, financial investment to sustain, or sacrifice to remain.

Life events themselves can also become training grounds. The death of a loved one, illness, marriage, parenting, career transitions, or seasons of loss all shape us in ways no classroom can. Wilderness moments, waiting periods, and obedience without explanation are often God's most intensive training environments, refining our trust, resilience, and faith.

If the area needing growth is spiritual, then the training ground must also be spiritual. This may mean studying the Word in community or under sound teaching instead of remaining isolated. It may require establishing a quiet place and set time for prayer, choosing consistency over crisis-driven spirituality. It may involve sitting under spiritual leadership rather than remaining self-directed. Spiritual fitness, like any other, requires intentional structure.

Some training grounds we must actively seek out, while others find us without invitation. Often, the place we least want to commit to is the very place growth and purpose begins.

It started with a simple decision. My husband and I wanted to get healthier, so we joined a gym. People at church began noticing the change, and soon our pastor encouraged us to share what we were doing.

We started small, inviting a few people to our home on Sunday evenings for workouts. But it quickly grew. As people saw results, they asked about nutrition, so we began coaching them on that too.

Before long, forty people were involved. The average weight loss was 20 pounds, with some losing 50 or more. Many gained strength, energy, and under their doctors' care were able to reduce medications. But our hearts were for more than physical fitness. We wanted people to be spiritually whole too.

What emerged became RP Fitness, a ministry focused not just on physical health, but spiritual growth. Each Sunday, we spent time in bible study before heading to the garage gym.

We watched people grow stronger in body and return to God in heart, falling in love with His Word again. Along the way, I wrote two books to support the journey: one for physical health and another for spiritual.

- *Taming Your MONSTER Appetite: Find a Healthy Lifestyle You Can Live With*
- *Relaying the Word: A 16-Week Trek Through the Bible With Friends*

What began as our own effort to get fit became something far greater. When we set out to find our training ground, we never imagined we'd later become one for others to grow stronger from the inside out.

Looking back, it's clear that transformation doesn't happen by accident. It happens by intention. Growth requires a place, a process, and a willingness to be shaped over time. Before anything changed in others, it first had to take root in us. And that same principle holds true for anyone seeking lasting change: you don't stumble into strength. You step into a training ground that builds it.

FIND YOUR TRAINING COMMUNITY

Recognize who's on the fitness journey with you. Knowing your training community matters because growth, endurance, and purpose are rarely sustained in isolation. The people you surround yourself with shape how you think, what you tolerate, and what you believe is possible. Your community influences your habits, your courage, and your spiritual temperature, often without you realizing it.

As you read through the following groups of people, begin to take an inventory of the people in your life. Identify those who are helpful for reaching new levels, those who would oppose your progress, those who draw your attention away from your own path, and those who are watching it all unfold. Notice the areas where you may have too many or too few and make adjustments where needed.

Your Tribe

God designed us for connection, accountability, and mutual strengthening, not lone survival. When you know your tribe, you know where you are safe to be honest, where you are challenged to grow, and where you are supported when the journey gets heavy.

Healthy tribes actively invest in one another. They speak truth with love, not flattery. They pray for each other and with each other. They celebrate victories and carry burdens during losses. Tribes provide accountability when someone is drifting, encouragement when someone is weary, and wisdom when someone is unsure. They sharpen one another through shared experiences, honest conversations, and a commitment to growth. Ecclesiastes 4:9–10 reminds us that two are better than one because if one of them falls, the other can help pull them up. In a strong tribe, no one is meant to struggle unseen.

Because tribes are powerful, discernment about who you allow into yours is essential. Scripture repeatedly warns that the wrong associations can quietly derail purpose. However, the goal is not isolation or superiority.

Proverbs 13:20 tells us to walk with the wise and become wise, for a friend of fools suffers harm. Recognize that not everyone is meant to have access to your inner circle. Some people are called to your life for a season, others for a purpose, and some not at all. Guard your tribe carefully, because the voices closest to you will either strengthen your faith or slowly pull you away from it.

Your tribe is your team. Every effective team is made up of different roles working toward the same goal. Teammates run with you; water carriers support you behind the scenes; coaches give direction and correction; trainers help you heal and strengthen; and ultimately, God sets the vision and defines the win. No championship team is built on talent alone; it's built on alignment, trust, and a shared commitment to growth. When each role functions properly, the team moves with purpose instead of chaos.

Team dynamics matter because progress is never the result of one person doing everything. A healthy team functions as a unit, not a hierarchy of importance. Teammates push one another, cover blind spots, and refuse to let someone quit when fatigue sets in. Coaches and teachers bring perspective, strategy, and accountability, and they often see things the player can't mid-game. Support roles may not be visible, but they sustain endurance. When a team operates well, strengths are multiplied and weaknesses are protected, allowing the whole group to advance further than any individual could alone.

Every role on the team is essential, and when one is missing, the consequences show up quickly. Without coaches, people rely on instinct instead of wisdom and often repeat avoidable mistakes. Without trainers, injuries go untreated and burnout becomes normal. Without supportive teammates, isolation creeps in and discouragement grows. Even something as simple as a water carrier matters, because without replenishment, exhaustion sets in and performance collapses. Teams don't usually fail because of lack of effort; they fail because critical roles were ignored, undervalued, or never filled.

Because your tribe is your team, there should be clear requirements for who is allowed on it. Team members must share core values, respect boundaries, and be committed to growth instead of comfort. They should be able to tell the truth without tearing you down and encourage you without enabling stagnation. Faithfulness, humility, teachability, and consistency matter more than charisma or shared history. Not everyone is qualified for proximity. The right team doesn't just support who you are today. They help you become who God is calling you to be.

Other Athletes

Look around. There are other people out there running their own races. They aren't competing against you, and your race doesn't depend on them. Not to sound too harsh, but God never asked you to beat someone else's calling. He asked you to be faithful with your own.

What we're really racing against is not other people, but our own preparation. No one outruns what they've trained for. If the farthest you've ever run in practice is one hundred yards, it's unrealistic to expect to finish strong in a 5K. The same is true in life. We race against our mental readiness, our physical conditioning, our spiritual depth, our financial discipline. When we fall behind, it's usually not because someone else was faster. It's because we didn't train for the distance we're trying to cover. Preparation always sets the ceiling for performance.

Everyone has their own lane or court, and wisdom is knowing where your boundaries are. Staying in your lane means focusing on what God assigned to you and refusing the distraction of what He assigned to someone else. Scripture reminds us to run with endurance the race that is set before us.[20] Not a race we chose, not

---

[20] Hebrews 12:1

a race we borrowed, but the one set before us. Paul echoes this and urges us to test our own work rather than compare ourselves to others, because each person carries their own responsibility.[21] Staying in bounds matters too; stepping outside your lane leads to disqualification, frustration, and exhaustion. Growth happens within the limits God designed, not outside of them.

Comparison is one of the quickest ways to leave your lane. When we compare, we start measuring our progress against someone else's highlight reel instead of our own preparation. This comparison distorts reality. It makes us impatient with our process and dismissive of our progress. It pulls our eyes off what we're training for and fixes them on someone else's finish line. Peace and progress return the moment we stop asking, "Why am I not where they are?" and start asking, "Am I training for where I'm going?"

Your Opponent

Just to reiterate… other athletes are not your *true* opponents even though their name may be on the point board. The Word of God says we wrestle not against flesh and blood, but against spiritual forces, powers of darkness, and evil influences working behind the scenes.[22] Our true opponent is the enemy.

So, who is our enemy? Our enemy, the devil, is not passive or imaginary. Scripture is clear that there is an organized, intentional opposition working against God's people. Jesus described the devil as a murderer and the father of lies.[23] He does not always appear as

---

21 Galatians 6:4–5
22 Eph 6:12
23 John 8:44

obvious evil; he often disguises himself as an angel of light,[24] deceiving through distortion rather than outright denial. Like a roaring lion, he prowls, watching for moments of vulnerability, seeking to devour.[25] He is also the tempter. And if he directly targeted Jesus, we shouldn't assume that we are exempt.

The devil and his agents actively work against us by sowing opposition, confusion, and resistance at critical moments. The enemy often positions himself near doors of opportunity. He exploits human weakness through empty promises that appeal to desire while entangling people again in bondage. Scripture also describes his use of traps and schemes designed to ensnare the proud, the impatient, or the unaware.[26] These are not random attacks; they are calculated efforts to hinder obedience, delay progress, and derail calling.

The Bible gives sobering examples of how the enemy deceives people who were otherwise positioned for purpose. Satan incited David to take a census by fueling his pride, leading to devastating consequences. Eve was deceived in the garden through subtle questioning of God's word and character. Judas had betrayal planted in his heart long before the act itself. Ananias allowed Satan to fill his heart with greed. These stories reveal a pattern: the enemy rarely forces disobedience; he persuades, entices, and rationalizes until compromise feels reasonable.

Victory is not found in ignoring the enemy, but in recognizing his tactics, standing firm in truth, and refusing to yield ground.

---

[24] 2 Corinthians 11:14
[25] 1 Peter 5:7–9
[26] Psalm 10:2 and 2 Timothy 2:26

The Crowd

Whether we notice it or not, there is always a crowd around our lives. It includes people quietly watching and learning from how we live, cheerleaders who celebrate every step forward, and critics or naysayers who try to discourage us when the road gets hard. Some watch because they're curious. Others watch because they're struggling with similar challenges and want to see if perseverance is possible. Our choices, responses, and endurance become a living testimony. We can either give the crowd permission to hope or unintentionally teach them to quit.

The crowd provides perspective and pressure for us at the same time. Cheerleaders remind us that we're not alone and that our effort matters. Their encouragement can carry us through moments when our own strength runs thin. Even the critics serve a purpose; they reveal where we may need thicker skin, deeper conviction, or greater focus. The presence of a crowd adds weight to our race; it reminds us that what we do matters beyond ourselves and that our faithfulness has reach.

We serve the crowd as well. We run not just for ourselves, but for those watching us. As Jackie Joyner-Kersee said, *"The greatest part of a record is knowing it will inspire someone to break it."*

Our obedience, growth, and perseverance create permission for others to pursue more. We model what it looks like to stay in the race when it's uncomfortable and uncertain. We don't apologize for growth just like butterflies don't apologize for outgrowing the cocoon. By becoming who we're called to be, we quietly invite others to believe they can too.

To become fit for purpose, we must identify those who surround us: our tribe, fellow athletes, our opponent, and the crowd. Knowing each role clearly helps us focus, run wisely, and finish strong.

Dial In
Your Training

Dialing in your training means moving from scattered effort to intentional alignment. Each area of your life functions like a gear in the system, and any misalignment can throw the whole system out of balance or sync.

As you work to bring things into alignment, there may be friction at first. Some parts may grind or feel out of place. Some gears are larger and create momentum for the smaller ones, while smaller gears turn faster yet produce subtler changes; still, their impact adds up.

The following goals are important gears that, when dialed in and properly aligned, will move you closer to becoming truly fit for purpose.

Become Able

Becoming able is about ability. At its core, ability is the capacity to do what is required when it is required.

Ability takes different forms, and each one matters. Following are the body-associated ones discussed herein.

- *Physical ability* involves strength, endurance, mobility, and energy. It's what your body can do and sustain.
- *Mental and emotional ability* includes clarity, focus, emotional regulation, wisdom, and resilience. It's the capacity to think, decide, and persevere.

Physically Able

Physical health refers to the overall state of your body and its ability to function properly, free from disease or unmanaged illness. It reflects how well your internal systems (such as the immune, digestive, cardiovascular, and metabolic systems) are working together. It's commonly measured through medical indicators and biomarkers, including blood pressure, cholesterol levels, blood glucose, body composition, and inflammatory markers, as well as routine medical tests and screenings. Subjective indicators also matter, such as consistent energy levels, quality of sleep, absence of chronic pain, and a general sense of bodily well-being.

Physical fitness, by contrast, refers to what your body can do. It is a measure of physical performance and capability, assessed through benchmarks such as strength, endurance, speed, flexibility, balance, and cardiovascular capacity. Fitness is often measured using metrics like muscle mass, VO_2 max, resting heart rate, flexibility tests, or performance markers such as running pace, lifting capacity, or stamina during activity. A physically fit person can perform daily tasks and physical challenges efficiently, with adequate energy and without excessive fatigue.

Health and fitness are not the same. It is possible to be healthy without being physically fit. For example, someone may eat well and maintain normal health markers but engage in little physical activity. The opposite is also true: a person can be highly fit yet not fully healthy. Elite or high-performance athletes, for instance, may demonstrate exceptional physical ability while struggling with overtraining, eating disorders, or chronic stress.

True physical "ability" is built by intentionally developing both physical health and physical fitness together. Following are some tips for increasing physical ability:

- *Commit to regular exercise.* Train mobility and flexibility alongside strength and endurance.
- *Improve your eating habits.* Fuel your body with proper nutrition as your foundation.
- *Drink water.* Staying well hydrated supports brain function, energy levels, circulation, and recovery.
- *Prioritize rest.* Consistent sleep restores your brain and body, improves focus and emotional regulation, strengthens immunity, and gives you the energy needed to show up fully for the day.
- *Reduce stress-evoking stimuluses.* Manage stress before it compounds and sets off chemical and hormonal cascades in the body.
- *Take time for recovery.* Proper recovery prevents injuries and allows your body time to repair.

- *Stay proactive with your health.* Get regular medical care, seek treatment for medical issues and nutrient deficiencies, engage in preventive screenings, and consider hormone optimization or replacement therapy when medically appropriate and approved by your physician.

Take ownership of your body's upkeep because ability doesn't happen by accident; it's built through daily, disciplined choices.

Mentally and Emotionally Able

Becoming able means that you need to have mental and emotional health too. A mentally and emotionally healthy person is more stable and less reactive. They are adaptable and recover faster from setbacks and stress. They are self-aware and choose to show up as their best self. They sustain healthy relationships. They make sound decisions without being driven by fear, impulse, or unresolved wounds. Rather than avoiding discomfort, a mentally fit person moves through it, feeling deeply without being ruled by emotion, and regaining focus and direction when life disrupts their balance.

Mental and emotional health is cultivated intentionally. Strength training isn't only for the body. A small mind is a dangerous mind, and an unchecked will is a timebomb. Sometimes we need to give our mind and will something difficult to do in order to grow them. Following are some tips for increasing mental and emotional ability:

- *Purposefully limit what you consume.* Guard your eyes and ears from negative media, conversations, and self-talk. Don't ruminate on your own negative thoughts and immediately replace them with truth.
- *Practice delayed gratification.* Don't immediately respond to texts, buy things, or satisfy impulses. Waiting builds self-control.

- *Practice your ability to focus.* Set a timer for several minutes and do one thing without distraction or multitasking. Or sit quietly to practice silence. These activities strengthen attention.

- *Fast from stimulation.* Not only from food but other things like social media, news, or entertainment. Teach your brain that it doesn't need constant dopamine.

- *Learn or memorize something new.* Studying new things like language, logic, or music creates new neural pathways. Saturate your mind with poems, Scripture, and/or quotes for encouragement.

- *Practice gratitude rather than complaining.* List three to five things daily you're thankful for. Focusing on gratitude rewires our outlook and reduces anxiety.

- *Discipline your decision-making.* Make small, low-stakes decisions quickly instead of overthinking.

- *Increase your emotional exposure.* Have hard conversations instead of avoiding them. Schedule them if you need to, so you won't feel caught off guard.

- *Intentionally practice boundaries.* Be like Nancy Reagan's 1980s anti-drug campaign and "Just Say No." And get comfortable with <u>not</u> following up with a long explanation or justification for your response.

Hard things don't weaken the mind—they forge it. When I did the 75 Hard challenge, I learned firsthand just how powerful the mind really is. The challenge requires 75 consecutive days of two workouts a day, strict nutrition, drinking a gallon of water, reading ten pages of a nonfiction book, and taking a progress photo; no compromises and no restarts. One slip-up and you start again at Day 1. I already knew I could accomplish anything I truly put my mind to, but what I didn't know was whether I could do it more than one day in a row. Each morning became a mental decision before it was ever a physical one. Some days my body was tired, some days my motivation was gone, but every day required discipline. That experience taught me that consistency is built-in moments of resistance, and that mental strength grows when you choose to keep going long after the excitement wears off.

Becoming mentally and emotionally healthier is a vital part of becoming fit for purpose. When your inner world is strong, you're better equipped to handle pressure, make wise decisions, and stay aligned with what God is calling you to do.

Become Provisioned

Money is a tool. But for what? For many people, it serves only as a dopamine fix, brought on by actions like frivolous impulse spending and gambling.

Money isn't the problem, though. The issue is society's lust for it.

> *For the love of money is a root of all kinds of evil. Some people, eager for money, have wandered from the faith and pierced themselves with many griefs.* 1 TIMOTHY 6:10 NIV

God created money to be a tool for us, not an item of worship. He clearly states we can't serve both Him and money.[27] Either we will love one and hate the other or be devoted to one and despise the other.

Managing finances wisely is a form of worship and responsibility, aligning with the biblical principle of being good stewards of God's blessings. God instructs us to faithfully manage money in a way that honors Him.

---

[27] Matthew 6:24 and Luke 16:13

Jesus told a story about a master who went away and entrusted three servants with different amounts of money. When he returned, two servants had multiplied the money they were given while one servant had buried his out of fear of losing it. The master rewarded the two successful servants but rebuked the fearful one, taking away what he had because he did nothing with it and giving it to the already successful ones. This story shows the importance of wisely investing and multiplying what God entrusts to us.

Becoming provisioned for purpose isn't about getting rich. We are called to be financially able, meaning prepared, positioned, and free enough to say yes when God calls. Following are some practical, purpose-aligned ways people can train to become financially fit.

- *Gain clarity in your spending.* Know where your money actually goes and track your spending honestly. Create a simple budget that reflects values, not just bills.
- *Eliminate unnecessary debt.* Develop a plan to reduce high-interest and consumer debt. Stop financing lifestyles you can't sustain.
- *Build financial margin.* Establish an emergency fund (even small, consistent savings). Avoid living paycheck to paycheck when possible.
- *Increase financial literacy.* Learn basic investing, retirement planning, and taxes. Gain an understanding of contracts, interest, and long-term consequences. Seek wise counsel instead of guessing.
- *Train for provision, not just income.* Develop skills, experience, and certifications that increase earning potential.
- *Practice contentment and restraint.* Resist comparison and lifestyle inflation. Learn to delay gratification and reduce impulse spending. Choose long-term freedom over short-term pleasure.

- *Build systems, not stress.* Automate savings and giving where possible. Create rhythms for financial review instead of crisis management. Order reduces anxiety.
- *Practice faithful giving.* Tithes and offerings are a commandment from the Lord and failure to comply brings dire consequences. For more information, check out Malachi 3:8–10, Leviticus 27:30, Deuteronomy 12:5–19, and Proverbs 3:9.

Financial fitness is built through systems, skills, and stewardship, not willpower alone. The right tools such as budgeting apps, interest calculators, micro-saving apps can reduce friction, create margin, and keep your finances aligned with your goals.

Financial tools are means, though, and not magic; they only work when they're used consistently. These tools don't replace discipline, but they make discipline easier, clearer, and far more sustainable as you move toward financial fitness.

Financial fitness is about readiness. When your finances are trained, they stop dictating your choices and start supporting your purpose. The goal is for money to serve the mission, not the other way around.

Become Equipped & Qualified

We don't have to feel ready when God asks us to do something. I know for me, most times I step forward feeling deeply inadequate or ill-prepared. Being or feeling fully equipped or qualified is not a prerequisite for being called upon. When God calls you up to the plate, He will equip you with the bat AND the skill to swing it and make an impact.

The Lord does not send people on a mission empty-handed. Throughout Scripture, God equips people who feel unable to accomplish what stands before them. Moses was apprehensive about his calling, so God placed a rod in his hand and Aaron by his side. The pattern is clear: with divine calling comes divine provision.

At the same time, we must do our part in becoming equipped. Spiritual dependence does not eliminate personal responsibility. We can't expect God to do everything for us. He supplies grace, but we must steward the growth.

2 Timothy 3:17 teaches that we are to be thoroughly equipped for every good work. That equipping may include gaining new skills, pursuing education, earning certifications, or seeking mentorship. Following are practical ways we can participate in our own equipping:

- *Know you're God-certified.* When God calls us to do something, we must remember that the call itself is a certification. When God asks us to step forward, His calling *is* His endorsement.
- *Become educated and skilled.* Education sharpens the tools God has already placed within you. What is it that you need to reach the next level? A new skill, expertise, or certification? Leadership development? Ministry training?
- *Rename the things in your life.* Names carry powerful influence and people are often formed by the labels they hear. Deliberately reframe the difficult areas of your life by naming them in a way that shapes a more positive response. For example, a final examination is not an obstacle but an opportunity to demonstrate learning.

You may not feel ready in the moment, and that's okay. In all truth of the matter, the question isn't "Am I fully equipped?" It's "Am I willing to be?"

Become Available

My favorite riddle is "What is the first thing God created according to the Bible?" Most people will say heaven and earth.

In the beginning God created the heaven and the earth. GENESIS 1:1 KJV

But the correct answer is time. You can't have an "In the beginning" without having time to distinguish first from second from last.

Unlike for earth, there is no beginning or ending in God because He is everlasting to everlasting. He exists outside of time. Then why did he create time in the first place? What's it for?

Time is a tool designed for humanity, a framework through which we measure the rhythm of our lives and the unfolding of our actions. Through time, we make sense of the natural world, observing the cycles of day and night, the seasons, and the movement of the stars.

Time serves as a mirror, reflecting the consequences of our choices and guiding us to evaluate the paths we take. It is a boundary: a limit placed on our mortal existence that shapes the urgency of our decisions and the opportunities we are given. It marks deadlines not just in worldly terms, but in spiritual terms as well, prompting reflection, accountability, and the pursuit of salvation. In this way, time is both a measuring stick and a motivator, calling us to live deliberately and purposefully within the span allotted to us.

Time is relative and subjective, though. One day on earth does not equate to one day on another planet, and one hour for a young boy is much longer than the same hour is for his grandfather. Everyone's perspective of time is different. Consider the mayfly that lives only one day. How many mayfly generations exist in a single lifetime of a human? To the fly, it must seem that humans live forever.

Time has a way of slipping through our fingers, not always because of how much of it we have, but because of how we experience it. Research shows that when we are engaged, focused, or stimulated, time feels like it moves quickly. On the contrary, when we are idle, distracted, or waiting, time drags. In other words, time doesn't just pass; it is perceived.

Businesses make use of this kind of research on the perception of time. Ever notice the lines for rides and attractions at amusement parks and how they are never straight? By having the lines fragmented into different segments, no one can see the whole length of the line, thereby reducing frustration with a long wait. Ever notice the signs that say, "Wait time from here is 1 hour"? That's because research also shows that telling customers how long they can expect to wait helps to reduce the feeling of wait time. Giving them snacks or interesting things to do or look at in the meantime can also help.

When we're immersed in something, a few hours of activity can feel like minutes. The danger is what we are immersed in. When we focus on trivial or inconsequential things (for example, video games), large portions of our lives can quietly be consumed without us realizing it. Sometimes this sort of downtime is needed for rest or coping. However repeated sessions of it can capture us in a web of addiction and pull us off the path of living a purpose-filled life.

Too much preoccupation with non-purposeful activity has deeper implications and speaks to how we steward our lives. We must learn to structure our lives in a way that keeps us engaged in what matters. Otherwise, time doesn't just pass, but it will get away from us, leaving us wondering where it went and what we have to show for it.

Becoming available has a lot to do with time management. Following are some tips to help.

- *Restore work-life balance.* Do an honest evaluation of where your time and energy are going. Prioritize what truly matters and structure your schedule to reflect those priorities and not just your obligations. Create space for rest and reflection.
- *Set boundaries and stick with them.* Establish different types of boundaries such as time boundaries (how you schedule your day), relational boundaries (who you allow access to your time and energy), and task boundaries (what you choose to take on or decline). Clearly communicate boundaries to others, but more importantly, honor them yourself. Say no to things that pull you out of zone and don't blur the lines.
- *Get into a routine.* Identify key anchors such as required morning, afternoon, evening, and weekly activities. Attach new habits to existing ones and adjust gradually rather than trying to overhaul everything at once.
- *Make the most of waiting.* Transform otherwise idle time such as commuting, standing in line, or waiting for an appointment into opportunities to learn, gain new skills, or reinforce personal growth. Plan for both expected and

unexpected waiting times and always have something on hand you can pull from.

- *Ask God to redeem time for you.* When time feels insufficient, don't rely on your own strength. Ask God to redeem the time for you. He can remove distractions, sharpen your focus, and give you supernatural efficiency to accomplish far more than seems possible. Once, under a tight deadline, I produced an hour's worth of writing in a single minute; impossible for me, but not with God.

- *Stop all the hurrying.* Urgency is a tactic of the enemy to steal our peace and rush us into choices without consulting God. When pressured to act quickly, pause for God's guidance. Slowing down to seek God won't cost us, because He is able to make up the difference and accomplish more through our obedience than our hurrying ever could.

- *Account for your time correctly.* Account for your time with the same intentionality as money, because once it's spent, it's gone. Leave margins for the unexpected and be mindful of time stealers.

Becoming available to God means intentionally creating time and space in your life so you can recognize and respond when He calls. If your time is constantly filled with distractions and overcommitments, you may miss opportunities to step into His purposes. When you make room for God, you position yourself to be used by Him at the right time and in the right way.

Become Connected

All of life is shaped by the connections we keep. Of course, our most important connection is with God, but we are also called to be meaningfully connected to family, friends, peers, and colleagues. These relationships influence our thinking, habits, and growth. Being intentional about whom we are connected to and how we show up in those relationships is essential to living a balanced and purpose-driven life.

Building a social network that truly works often requires honest evaluation and intentional change. Some relationships may need healing through forgiveness, honest conversation, or restored trust, while others may need to be released if they consistently hinder growth or pull us away from our path. At the same time, it may be necessary to build new connections, especially with professionals, mentors, or like-minded individuals who can challenge and sharpen us.

> *Iron sharpens iron, and one man sharpens another.* PROVERBS 27:17 ESV

It's important to surround ourselves with each of these three key roles: one up, one over, and one down. A "one up" person is a mentor, someone ahead of us who offers wisdom, guidance, and perspective. A "one over" is a peer, someone walking alongside us who provides accountability, encouragement, and shared growth. A "one down" is someone we are pouring into, offering guidance, support, and what we've learned along the way. If there is a vacancy or insufficient coverage in any of these roles, we need to acknowledge and rectify.

Following are some places to become connected.

- *Faith communities.* Connect with churches, bible studies, prayer groups, or spiritual mentorship programs where members can grow spiritually and be encouraged in their walk with God.
- *Professional networks.* Join industry associations, conferences, or online professional groups to access mentorship opportunities.

- *Educational communities.* Enroll in colleges, workshops, certification or training programs, or online courses to find people walking a similar path.
- *Local or civic groups.* Join volunteer organizations, community service groups, or local clubs to find people who can broaden one other's perspective.
- *Social or peer circles.* Surround yourself with friends, peers, or groups who hold one another accountable, provide encouragement, and share common goals or interests.

Become connected by building relationships that align with your purpose, strengthen your character, and help you both give and receive in meaningful ways.

Become Prioritized & Aligned

Without clear, aligned foundational priorities, your life will be shaped by whatever demands the most attention. And the danger goes beyond wasted time, wasted energy, and wasted life. Imagine reaching the end of your life only to realize you led the generation following you down that same misguided road. Don't let another day go by without making sure you have the correct foundational priorities in life and that you're aligned with them.

Deciding what your priorities are in life often begins with deep and honest reflection to consider what truly matters to you. It can help to ask yourself questions like: "What brings me fulfillment?" or "What kind of legacy do I want to leave?" or "What kind of person do I want to be?" Sometimes the questions are easier to answer with the help of trusted comrades who can offer perspective and accountability.

When our lives are correctly prioritized and aligned, it's much like a well-functioning computer running smoothly according to its programs and sequence of operations. Just as a computer will process tasks in the right order, allocating memory and resources efficiently, we operate best when our values, roles, and responsibilities are clearly ordered and in harmony. Misaligned priorities are like software glitches or conflicting programs: they slow us down, create stress, and cause errors in judgment. And just like computers, sometimes we just need some personal IT support.

- *Time to close some apps.* Close the nonessential things going on in the background that are slowing you down and stealing your focus. And are there things open that may be unacceptable to God? Close them too. Close them right now.
- *Time to delete the browsing history.* Sometimes opening into a new tab in life requires clearing out the past.
- *Time to get powered* ON. If you don't know Jesus as your Savior, then take a leap of faith and let Him power you on with everlasting life. And if you do, ask Him for a fresh filling of His Holy Spirit to bring renewed power into your life.
- *Time for a restart.* Sometimes we just need a restart in life. This might look like a new job, a move to another city, or simply joining a gym.
- *Time for a shutdown.* A shutdown is different than a restart. Sometimes you just need a good shutdown like sleep or a vacation get-away. Avoid bad shutdowns like unhealthy escapes or chemical dependencies.
- *Time to pull out the operating manual.* Use your God-given manual, the Bible, to decide things like how to handle a difficult conversation with a family member, manage your priorities, or respond to a stressful situation.

Don't wait until everything in your life crashes to check your priorities. Like a computer that suddenly freezes when it's overloaded, our lives can reach a breaking point when too many distractions, obligations, or misaligned choices pile up. Waiting until that moment of total frustration only makes recovery harder. Instead, regularly assess what matters most, close what's unnecessary, and keep your focus on what truly counts.

Become Single-Minded

I grew up in the late 1980s, so like other Generation X-ers, I watched A LOT of television. My favorites were game shows, especially The Hollywood Squares.

The overall premise of this game show was tic-tac-toe with a celebrity occupying each square. My favorites were Wayland Flowers and Madame, Weird Al Yankovic, Charo, Jonathan Winters, and most of all, Joan Rivers. I spent hours watching the show.

The gameplay was simple. A contestant would choose a celebrity to answer a trivia question. The contestant would then decide whether the answer was true or not, and if they assessed correctly, they won the square. But here's where the fun comes in. The celebrities were coached prior to the show on how to give bluff answers that were plausible but untrue. For each answer the celebrities gave during the show, they would provide the rationale for their choice, often weaving these extravagant stories designed to confuse the contestants.

The goal for the celebrity was to sow seeds of doubt and confusion in the contestants. It was common to see a contestant, who knew the answer straight up, change their mind because of some encyclopedic-sounding answer that was total bunk. Those celebrities could literally talk a contestant out of knowing the name of their own first-born child.

Basically, the game exploited the human nature to doubt. And while double-mindedness in this game was quite entertaining, in real life, it can be catastrophic.

So, what is double-mindedness, really?

When we talk about double-mindedness, we're not talking about having multiple opinions. An opinion is a personal viewpoint or judgment about something. Double-mindedness means being internally divided, wanting two *opposing* things at once. It's like trying to wear two jerseys and play for both teams at once; it doesn't work, and eventually you'll be forced to decide whose side you're really on.

Double-mindedness is doubt and belief trying to occupy the same space. It's worry and faith attempting to coexist. It's believing something is possible but not for you. You can have limits or you can have the Lord, but you can't have them both.

Following are steps you can take to eradicate double-mindedness and become single-minded.

- *Make a choice in what you believe.* As the old saying goes, if you don't stand for something, you'll fall for anything. Decide on your convictions and hold fast, letting them guide every thought and action. If you need help with this, see my book *Make a Choice.*
- *Know who you are and who you want to be.* Scripture says you are a child of the King, and that identity should anchor every

other role you carry. Ask yourself where in your life you may be experiencing an identity crisis or where you are acting out of character. Be honest with yourself in all these answers and decide who you *really* want to be, then be it.

- *Have the mind of Christ.* Take responsibility for your thought life and don't surrender it to anxiety, intimidation, or defeat. For me, this becomes especially real after I speak publicly, and self-doubt tries to replay every flaw or imagined criticism. The enemy's whispers can be sharp and relentless, but I've learned to recognize the pattern and refuse agreement. Having the mind of Christ isn't passive; it's a deliberate, daily decision to renew your mind, reject lies, and stand firm in truth.

- *Use subjection.* Subjection is the deliberate act of bringing your body, mind, and emotions under control instead of letting them control you. It retrains your responses so that you no longer react automatically to every impulse, mood, or trigger, but instead align yourself with what you know is right. If you want to learn more about subjection, including actual ways to do it, see my book *Subject Your Flesh: Stop Being a Victim of Your Destructive Desires.*

- *Persist and sustain.* Change isn't secured in a single victory; it's maintained through steady reinforcement. Like any training process, replacing old habits with new ones requires consistency; without reinforcement, old patterns quietly creep back in. This is where subjection matures into lifestyle. It's not just about taking control in a heated moment; it's about sustaining that control through daily practice.

Become Aware

God designed us to be like living antennas, constantly receiving signals through multiple channels including eyes, ears, gut, touch, smell, sense, etc. We were created with these gates on purpose to discern our environment, respond wisely to what surrounds us, evade danger, and remain attuned to both physical realities and spiritual truth. But because these gates are always active, they must be guarded. Every conversation, image, tone, and idea that passes through these gates leaves an imprint. If we are careless about what we permit to enter through, then we shouldn't be surprised by what begins to form within us.

Awareness matters because it sharpens discernment. When you are attentive, you interpret situations more accurately, choose wiser responses, and close the gates that are too widely open. We must avoid being subtly shaped by influences we never intend to adopt, because we, as humans, are natural imitators.

Researchers at the University of California explored how easily humans slip into unconscious imitation.[28] In the study, normal-hearing participants with no lip-reading training watched a silent video of a person speaking a series of words. After each word, the participants were asked to say aloud what they believed had been spoken. They were never instructed to mimic the person on the screen. Yet the results showed that when participants voiced the words they had lip-read, their speech subtly took on the patterns of the silent speaker. In fact, their pronunciation more closely resembled the unseen talker's style than when they simply read the same words from a printed list. The study demonstrated how naturally and unintentionally we mirror others, even without conscious effort.

---

[28] Dias JW, Rosenblum LD. Visibility of speech articulation enhances auditory phonetic convergence. Atten Percept Psychophys. 2016;78(1):317-33.

Just as our minds and mouths can unconsciously mirror others, our hearts and choices require intentional guidance to align with God's truth. The following are practical, biblical ways to sharpen your awareness and steward the gateways God has given you.

- *Wake up.* Waking up means choosing to not sleepily drift through life on autopilot. It is a call to rise from passivity and engage life in all its fullness. We must be alert and active if we expect to be able to respond immediately when we sense a need.

- *Guard your eyes and ears.* First impressions form quickly. In fact, it takes less than two-tenths of a second for someone to form a first impression.[29] Scripture warns to not place wicked things before our eyes or listen only to what our "itching ears" want to hear.[30] While it is important to guard our senses, we must also strike a balance so that we don't close the gates completely, lest we become blind and deaf to what God has for us.

- *Be sober-minded.* The Bible tells us to be sober-minded and watchful.[31] When folks hear the word sobriety, they tend to think only of drugs and alcohol, but it's actually much broader than that. We must stay both physically and spiritually sober, being clear-minded and watchful.

- *Do a sound check.* Doing a "sound check" is a helpful way to become aware of the atmosphere we are either creating or absorbing. If the sound is not aligned with peace, gratitude, and wisdom, then it is a signal to refocus attention, adjust influences, and choose speech that reflects the character we want to cultivate.

- *Be quick to listen, slow to speak.* Scripture says to be swift to hear, slow to speak, slow to wrath.[32] Speaking out of

---

[29] https://www.newswise.com/articles/first-impressions-form-quickly-on-the-web-eye-tracking-study-shows
[30] Psalm 101:3 and Isaiah 33:15
[31] 1 Peter 5:8
[32] James 1:19

impulse or emotion can lead to unnecessary conflict or words that can never be taken back. Cultivating this habit requires patience, humility, and the willingness to value understanding over the urge to immediately be heard.

- *Test everything.* Exercise wisdom and discernment rather than accepting ideas without careful evaluation. Compare thoughts, advice, cultural messages, and personal impulses against biblical truth rather than following them simply because they are popular or emotionally appealing.

- *Increase your focus.* Golfers use the "Quiet Eye" technique, where they briefly alternate their gaze between the ball and the target, then hold a steady, focused look before and during the stroke. The principle of steadying your aim applies beyond sports. When life feels like repeated "putting" without making progress, increase your focus to move through the challenges more efficiently.

Awareness is a foundational gear in the larger design of becoming truly fit for purpose. In the overall plan, awareness is what keeps the system calibrated; it ensures that your thoughts, choices, and actions move in harmony with God's intent. When you live aware, you live aligned, and alignment is what allows purpose to gain traction and move forward with power.

BE OKAY
WITH DOWN TIMES

Downtimes are a normal and unavoidable part of life. Scripture reminds us in Ecclesiastes 3:1–8 that there is a season for everything. These seasons may show up as physical injury or illness, emotional burnout, loss of motivation, or unexpected interruptions. Sometimes they are personal, like family crises or grief; other times they are external and uncontrollable, such as severe weather, natural disasters, economic upheaval, or even global pandemics.

Downtimes don't mean failure. They mean we are human, living within rhythms that God designed.

The most important thing *to do* during a downtime is to listen to your body, your circumstances, and to God. This is a season for recovery, reflection, and wise adjustment, not self-condemnation.

The most important thing *to NOT do* is to quit altogether or interpret the pause as the end of your calling. Downtime is not disqualification; it is often preparation. What you resist in frustration, you may miss in formation.

How to Wait Actively Instead of Striving

Have you ever tried to push a car off the road? Remember how difficult it was to turn the wheels without the car moving? Clearly, it's harder to steer a parked car than one that's moving.

Forward momentum (even slow, imperfect movement) creates the ability to adjust direction. If we keep moving, even if it's a slow creep, God will have an easier time steering us into the right direction.

We are called to stay active, engaged, and alert, not idle or asleep at the wheel. Waiting does not mean stopping. It means moving wisely while watching closely.

Active waiting is purposeful movement under God's direction, while striving is frantic motion fueled by fear, impatience, or control. The apostle Paul captures this distinction when he says, *"I do not run like someone running aimlessly; I do not fight like a boxer beating the air."*[33] Striving is like boxing the air (lots of effort with no target), whereas active waiting keeps form, posture, and focus, even when the outcome isn't immediate. One is disciplined and intentional; the other is exhausting and ineffective.

Learn to move with patience, not pressure. Patience allows us to move at the pace of obedience rather than the pace of anxiety. Pressure pushes us to hurry outcomes God is still forming. When

---

[33] 1 Corinthians 9:26 NIV

we learn to move with patience, we remain faithful in small steps, trusting that consistency matters more than speed.

Don't push forward in panic. Panic-driven progress often leads to poor decisions, wrong timing, and veering off course. When fear takes the wheel, we may rush into relationships, careers, commitments, or spiritual assignments before we are prepared or called. The cost of moving too fast can be just as damaging as not moving at all.

Waiting actively means staying faithful to what is in front of you while remaining open to what God is preparing next. It looks like continuing to serve with excellence even when promotion hasn't come, maintaining healthy habits while results are still invisible, and showing up consistently in prayer and the Word instead of only seeking God in crisis. Active waiting may involve training, learning, saving, healing, or strengthening character. It could be quiet work that doesn't feel dramatic but builds readiness. It is choosing obedience today, rather than impatience tomorrow, trusting that steady faithfulness keeps you positioned for the moment when the new door finally opens.

Trust God in the space between action and fulfillment means doing what you know to do today while leaving tomorrow in His hands. Fulfillment may be delayed, but it is never wasted when your steps are aligned with Him.

When You Need Some Rehab and Recovery

God rests. And He commands us to do so too.

From the very beginning, rest is woven into God's design. After creation, God rested, not because He was tired, but because rest completes good work. He then commanded His people to rest as well, establishing a rhythm meant to sustain life, not interrupt it.

Rest is necessary for both the body and the mind. Physically, rest allows muscles to repair, hormones to regulate, and energy to be restored. Mentally and emotionally, rest quiets overstimulation, sharpens focus, and prevents burnout. Without intentional rest, we don't become stronger; we become depleted. Rest is not the enemy of productivity; it is what makes long-term effectiveness possible.

The Sabbath represents complete and intentional rest. It is a set-apart time when no work is done. God created the Sabbath for our benefit, not as a burden. As Jesus said, *"The Sabbath was made for man, not man for the Sabbath."*[34] It is a holy pause that reminds us we are not sustained by effort alone, but by God.

At the same time, the holy Sabbath is distinct from other forms of rest. Not all sabbaths look like a single day on a calendar. Sometimes rest comes in longer stretches, what we often call sabbaticals, which are seasons intentionally set aside for renewal, recalibration, or healing. These extended rests honor the same principle but apply it over a broader span of time.

There are also seasons when we need to recover, rehab, and rebuild. These are not times of complete stillness like the Sabbath, but forms of active recovery. We may still be moving forward, just at a different pace, allowing strength to return while avoiding further injury or exhaustion. Growth continues here, but gently.

Rest is not always about the body alone. We may need emotional rest from constant pressure, mental rest from decision fatigue, or

---

[34] Mark 2:27 KJV

spiritual rest from striving. Sometimes rest looks like increased fellowship with God rather than increased output. Other times, it means sitting still and allowing God to work without our interference. Zechariah experienced this when God silenced him, saying that he would be silent until the appointed time.

Rest is not weakness. It is both obedience and wisdom built into becoming fit for purpose. Scripture tells us that anyone who enters God's rest also rests from their works, just like God did from His.[35] When we rest as God intended, we don't fall behind. Instead, we align ourselves with His rhythm, and that alignment is where true strength is formed.

If you find yourself in a season of rest, your assignment is not to rush through it, explain it away, or feel guilty about it. Receive rest as a gift, not a punishment. Pay attention to what is being restored and what is being revealed. This is a time to listen more than speak, to heal what has been strained, and to allow God to recalibrate your desires and direction. Stay connected to Him through prayer, Scripture, and quiet obedience, even if outward productivity is low. Rest seasons are not empty; they are formative. What you allow God to restore in you now will determine how well you carry what comes next.

When Closing Doors Feel Like the End

For those times when you sense a door closing in your life, don't dwell on what's ending. Instead, lift your eyes and watch for the

---

[35] Hebrews 4:10

doors God *is opening.* Even when our plans seem blocked, He will redirect our paths and guide us toward the future He has prepared.

In their hearts humans plan their course, but the Lord establishes their steps. PROVERBS 16:9 NIV

Closed doors don't always stay closed. Sometimes, God will allow them to open again.

Some years ago, I knew without a doubt that God was closing the door to me being a writer. Now this was huge because being a writer wasn't just what I did, but it was WHO I was. I've been writing since about 1998. But recently, I had strayed in the kinds of writing I was doing and stepped over the line into secular writing that I knew in my heart was not God-approved. I knew I was no longer fit for purpose.

I awoke one day in April assuming it was just another Thursday. I had no idea this would actually be the day God would say "no more." Although it was the hardest thing I have ever had to do in my life, I stopped writing. I didn't give up my fulltime job of writing for pharmaceutical companies because this writing didn't belong to me, but I did surrender all my personal writing. This was hard because it was how I untangled my thoughts and emotions. How I cleared my head. How I released the creative energy balled up inside me. To give it up was death. I seriously felt a part of myself literally die. I grieved deeply, and I completely let go of the hope of ever writing again. When ideas for writing came, I ignored them.

About halfway through the grieving, I actively made a decision to turn my attention toward finding my fitness. Looking for answers, I attended a Christian retreat where I recommitted my life to Christ and His Kingdom, I got rebaptized and created a bracelet to wear daily as a permanent reminder to pray and seek the true North. On the corded bracelet was a metal washer with the engraved words "Fit for Purpose." I knew in my heart that when the cord broke on its own that I would be fit enough to enter the next season God was preparing me for, whatever that may be. I forbade myself to dream about the possibility of writing again and vowed it dead unless I was worthy enough to be released to it again.

The following year, the bracelet cord broke on its own unexpectedly. These sorts of seasons can vary in length for folks, but for me it lasted 408 days and 20 hours, and I felt every second of it. During this time, I had to completely surrender and let a piece of my life and identity succumb to a death. It wasn't until afterward that I felt the transformation. I had been a caterpillar, and what the caterpillar calls the end, God calls a rest stop.

Through the weeks and months afterwards, I began to sense a release to write again. And this book, which lay dormant for years, was finally birthed out of it.

If you find yourself in a season where doors seem to be slamming in your face, don't give up. I know it's cliché, but the simplicity of it is so true. There is a reason this is happening to you, and it's meant for your own good. Sometimes God closes many doors so you'll stop running between them and stand still long enough to notice certain ones. Hold your ground, guard your hope, and remember: a closed door is not a verdict; it's often a redirection. And not all closed doors will remain closed.

How to Regain Perspective

Downtimes have a way of quietly shifting our perspective if we're not careful. What begins as honest reflection can slowly turn into unhealthy questioning like: Why did this happen? Who's at fault? and eventually slide into blame, denial, or discouragement. This is especially true when the downtime is the result of our own choices, actions, or lack thereof. Shame can creep in, distorting the story we tell ourselves, until we start believing that this pause defines us rather than refines us.

It's critical to guard against letting past "mistakes" or irreversible outcomes convince us that trying again isn't worth it. We can't undo the past, but we also aren't sentenced to live there. When things don't unfold as planned, regret and doubt often compete for control of our thinking. Left unchecked, they can drain curiosity, kill momentum, and keep us from re-engaging with purpose.

Perspective matters. When it begins to drift, we must intentionally pull it back before discouragement settles in.

One of the best ways to get back on track is to remember. Recall moments when you persevered, when God carried you through something that should have taken you out, or when growth came after difficulty. Revisit past victories, not to live in them, but to remind yourself that you are capable and that God is faithful. Sometimes progress starts simply by changing how we're looking at the situation. A new vantage point can turn a setback into a setup and restore the courage to move forward again.

> .evitcepsrep tuoba lla s'tI
>
> Sometimes we just need to see it from a different point of view.

When I was a teenager, a friend and I thought fun meant pushing our luck. We loved to speed down one-lane country roads with hairpin curves. We'd even time our trek and try to beat it again and again.

One summer day, we flew around a blind curve at about 50 mph and suddenly faced an oncoming tractor. There was no room to slow down or swerve; a deep creek ran alongside the road.

The tractor was pulling a farm implement that stretched across the road at head level. I braced myself, certain we were about to be decapitated. I watched it reach the windshield, *and then somehow*, pass through without touching us. We pulled over in shock and inspected the car. Not a scratch. No explanation.

I had a choice to make that day: tell the story of how my life was spared and then be forced to change the way I was living in appreciation or let the memory of the event die in my place.

For over twenty years, the story lay dormant in forgotten memories until the moment God knew I needed to be reminded. That day, I kept recounting an unsettling dream I'd had the night before about someone calling my mom and asking about me and my family. Later that day, my mom received a strange call from no other than the person in my dream. This person, who suffered from mental illness, revealed that he was "told" to cut off my head. The conversation she described included all the things I had heard in my dream the night before.

The moment my mom finished describing the disturbing exchange, I heard the Lord speak very clearly to me: "I saved you once from having your head cut off and I can do it again." IMMEDIATELY, the story about the tractor was resurrected in my mind in clear detail.

I couldn't decide what was more amazing—that someone wanted to cut off my head <u>or</u> that I could have forgotten such a miraculous story <u>or</u> that I dreamed about the conversation before it happened <u>or</u> that the Lord was speaking directly to me. The one thing I had no trouble deciding, though, was that God was at work in my life.

Our Heavenly Father has a plan for our life: plans to prosper us and not to harm us; plans to give us hope and a future.[36]

Although there was a hit out on me (not once, but twice), Jesus paid the price on my head. And He paid it for you, too. Sometimes we just need to be reminded so we can regain the right perspective.

How to Be at Peace With It All

Many people struggle to find peace in becoming fit for purpose. It's rarely the hard work itself that daunts them. More often, they resist the direction they're headed or claim not to know where they're supposed to be. In reality, the truth is often simpler: they *do* know their purpose… they just don't like it because it may not seem glamorous, impressive, or worthy of attention. People want to be seen, heard, and immediately recognized; they crave instant credit for their efforts. Truly being at peace with it all requires us to

---

[36] Jeremiah 29:11

surrender ideas of applause and popularity. We must embrace purposes for our life that may seem less prestigious on the surface. A perfect example of this is parenting.

Parenting may be the single most important purpose we have on earth. (And yes, even childless people can still have opportunities to parent/mentor through wonderful, nonprofit organizations.) By guiding children, shaping their character, and modeling faith, we plant seeds that can ripple far beyond ourselves and touch families, communities, and even generations to come. Every small act of instruction, discipline, or encouragement carries eternal significance, even when it feels mundane, frustrating, or unnoticed. The faith and testimony we instill may inspire our children to accomplish things we could never imagine or have the opportunity to do, impacting lives long after we are gone. If what we sow today empowers someone else to do something world-changing tomorrow, we have indeed fulfilled a divine purpose.

Yet parenting is often underestimated. It's easy to discount the importance of nurturing the next generation, even though this may be the most critical mission God entrusts to us. Many people struggle to grasp the idea of investing an entire lifetime without seeing the full fruits of their labor. Time spent pouring into children and grandchildren may never bear visible reward during our lives. We may never have a world-wide ministry or public recognition, but if all God asks of us is to disciple and nurture the next generation, can we accept that? Can we see the greatness of purpose in something so quiet, so unseen, yet so profoundly influential?

Parenting isn't the only example here. For example, think about Rosie the Riveters. They likely had no idea at the time just how pivotal their daily, repetitive work would be. Day after day, they riveted, hammered, and assembled planes, tanks, and munitions, performing tasks that seemed monotonous and mundane. Most were focused simply on showing up, doing their job, and supporting their families while the men were at war. Yet each bolt tightened and each part secured contributed directly to the Allied war effort, keeping the machinery of victory moving. What seemed ordinary in the moment (a routine, laborious job), ultimately became extraordinary, proving that faithful effort, even in tasks that feel small or invisible, can change the course of history.

There are other examples of overlooked purpose that seem small or inconsequential but carry high stakes. Serving quietly behind the scenes, caring for a neighbor, volunteering in small ways: these may feel minor, yet the impact can ripple far beyond what we see.

To find peace in the process of becoming fit for purpose, sometimes we must shift our mindset by looking for the eternal value, not the immediate applause. Ask God to show you how even small actions may contribute to a larger plan. Seek to align your efforts with what truly matters in His eyes, and you'll find significance in places you once thought were trivial. Purpose often hides in the ordinary; learning to see it there will bring peace to your heart and mind.

KNOW THE COST
BEFORE YOU START

Everything has a cost. Period.

Before we begin the journey of becoming fit for purpose, we must be honest about the cost. This is the moment to take off the rose-colored glasses and put on our accounting hat. Purpose is not entered into casually or emotionally; it requires sober evaluation. Jesus Himself warned us to count the cost before building or going to war, because unfinished work and abandoned callings leave us frustrated and discouraged. Clarity up front doesn't kill faith; it strengthens it by anchoring our expectations in reality rather than fantasy.

> *Suppose one of you wants to build a tower. Won't you first sit down and estimate the cost to see if you have enough money to complete it? For if you lay the foundation and are not able to finish it, everyone who sees it will ridicule you, saying, "This person began to build and wasn't able to finish."* LUKE 14:28–30 NIV

The costs of becoming fit for purpose come in many forms. Some are tangible, like finances, time, energy, education, or even relocation. Others are less visible but just as real: strained relationships, misunderstood motives, delayed gratification, physical exhaustion, emotional weariness, and seasons of isolation. Some costs are things we actively incur (i.e., sacrifices we choose to make), while others are circumstances we must endure, such as opposition, loss, waiting, or being overlooked. Purpose often demands that we give up what is comfortable for what is necessary.

When we fail to consider these costs, disillusionment quickly follows. We may interpret hardship as failure rather than confirmation that the process is working. Unexpected resistance can tempt us to quit, blame God, or assume we missed our calling altogether. Ignoring the cost doesn't make it disappear; it just ensures we'll be unprepared when the bill comes due. Many people abandon purpose not because they weren't called, but because they never correctly anticipated the price of answering that call.

As we go forward, it's important to examine these potential costs more closely, while also recognizing that not every cost can be foreseen. Understanding what may be required helps us stand firm when challenges arise and keeps us from being shaken by what was always part of the process. When we acknowledge the cost ahead of time, we can commit with open eyes, steady resolve, and a deeper trust that God will supply the grace needed for every step.

Obstacles in Your Path

When the Israelites stood on the edge of the Promised Land, God was clear about what lay ahead. He instructed Israel to drive out completely the seven nations already occupying the land. God never hid the fact that taking possession requires confrontation. The promise was real, but so was the resistance. Taking the land would demand a battle cost.

For us today, these seven nations are not people we must confront but are symbols of what stands in the way of us becoming fit for purpose. They represent deep-rooted obstacles that already occupy the territory God intends for our growth. We must kill the root of these issues, not the symptoms themselves.

- *Fear and intimidation.* Fear of failure, fear of people, fear of change. These loom large and make us shrink back before we even start.
- *Comfort and complacency.* The pull to stay where it's familiar. Not sinful, just numbing. Comfort that keeps us from moving forward.
- *Pride and self-reliance.* The belief that we know better, or that we can do this in our own strength. Pride resists correction and growth.
- *Compromise and material distraction.* Being driven by money, success, image, or productivity at the expense of calling and character.
- *Lack of boundaries and discipline.* Living unguarded, unfocused, and reactive. Everything gets access, so nothing gets depth.
- *Deception and half-truths.* Subtle lies we believe about ourselves or God: "This is just how I am," "God understands if I quit," "I'll deal with it later."
- *Old strongholds and identity wounds.* Long-standing habits, past failures, trauma, or labels that say, "This is who you've always been."

Taken together, these "nations" show us something important: becoming fit for purpose isn't just about adding new habits or skills. It's about removing what already occupies the land. God was clear with Israel that He would not drive their enemies out in a single day, lest the land become desolate and new problems arise before they were ready. Growth had to match their capacity to steward what was gained. In the same way, the things that oppose our purpose are often removed gradually, not instantly, so we can develop strength, wisdom, and endurance along the way. And just like Israel, we don't overcome everything in one decisive battle. This day-by-day progress carries an additional cost: consistent obedience, sustained effort, and the patience to keep showing up when breakthroughs feel slow.

The man who removes a mountain begins by carrying away small stones.
WILLIAM FAULKNER

The Pain of Change

Physical pain is a signal, a built-in alert system that something in our body or life requires attention. It warns us when we're pushing too hard, when something is wrong, or when growth is underway. Without it, we might ignore necessary adjustments or push too far past our abilities.

The pain of change is no different. Just as muscle growth requires micro-tears, inflammation, and repair, becoming fit for purpose requires daily resistance and small battles that strain us first, so that real strength can be built afterward. This process is inherently uncomfortable, but the discomfort signals transformation, adaptation, and progress.

Ask a pruned tree how it feels in the moment, and you'll understand the purpose of temporary discomfort. Pain will come, and sometimes it may be intense, but can also be very productive.

Some pain is acute, like childbirth, but some is chronic. Pain changes over time and we can acquire a tolerance to it. Patients undergoing repeated medical tests or treatments often report that what once felt unbearable becomes manageable. The body and mind adapt, teaching us resilience, endurance, and confidence in our capacity to handle what comes.

Embracing pain, rather than medicating or masking it, is essential to growth. When we avoid feeling it, we risk missing the lessons it carries and stunting the strength it is meant to build. If we cover pain in general, we also risk missing the specific signals our body or life is sending about areas that need attention. Masking pain may give temporary relief, but it prevents the transformation that only discomfort can produce, leaving us weaker and unprepared for the challenges ahead. Sometimes, we just need to grit our teeth and get through it.

Mentally preparing for the cost of pain is just as important as enduring it physically. Knowing that growth, change, and purpose often come with discomfort allows us to face it with intention rather than fear. It means accepting that the struggle is not a sign of failure, but a necessary part of the process. I experienced this firsthand during natural labor and delivery. Although I had prepared my mind for it, when it came time, I still had to give myself permission to feel it fully, knowing that enduring it was part of the process of bringing new life into the world.

Like an athlete anticipating sore muscles after a hard workout, we can brace ourselves emotionally and spiritually for the pushbacks, setbacks, or resistance that will inevitably come. By acknowledging the cost ahead of time, we empower ourselves to persist through it.

All Talk, No Action

Talking about something isn't enough. Even the best intentions carry no weight unless they are acted upon. Without the actual doing part, our words are empty promises to ourselves and to God.

In the parable of the two sons, one son initially refuses his father's request but later obeys, while the other agrees but never acts. Jesus makes it clear that true obedience is measured not by what we say, but by what we actually do.

> *Not everyone who says to me, "Lord, Lord," will enter the kingdom of heaven, but only the one who does the will of my Father who is in heaven.*
> MATTHEW 7:21 NIV

Procrastination can be a temporary delay but failing to act when we knowingly should is a moral and spiritual failure.

Some people think that indecision is the same as inaction. But, it's not. *Not making a decision is still a decision.* It's a decision to not do the thing. Let that sink in.

Taking action always carries a cost. It demands energy, courage, time, and the willingness to be seen trying and possibly failing. It may cost comfort, predictability, or approval from others. Once you act, you can no longer hide behind intentions, excuses, or "someday." Action exposes what you truly believe and value because it puts skin in the game. But while the cost of action is real and often uncomfortable, the cost of inaction is usually far greater.

The Tomorrow Trap

Living in the today means fully engaging with the moment God has placed before us. Scripture repeatedly reminds us of the importance of today: *"This is the day the Lord has made; let us rejoice and be glad in it"* and *"Do not boast about tomorrow, for you do not know what a day may bring."*[37] We cannot keep saying, "I'll start tomorrow" or "Next week." How often do diets or goals start on Mondays, as if the universe pauses to accommodate our procrastination? This is what I call the "tomorrow trap"—a cycle of endless delays that keeps us from moving forward.

The enemy thrives in the tomorrow trap. He whispers doubts, magnifies obstacles, and convinces us of all the reasons we can't start. "You don't have enough time. You aren't ready. You'll fail." His goal is simple: keep us frozen in indecision so God's purposes remain unfulfilled in our lives.

Some call it stalling and other procrastination. The bottom line is we stall when we replace action with excuses. How long is too long? When we continually justify inaction to ourselves, others, or even God, we've crossed the line from careful planning to self-deception. Stalling looks like busy work, constant preparation, or waiting for perfect circumstances, but deep down, we know it's avoidance.

The longer we remain trapped in "tomorrow," the more opportunity passes us by. Years can slip away while we wait for perfect conditions, leaving dreams unfulfilled, skills undeveloped, and purpose delayed. Momentum is never regained by wishing; it is gained by stepping into today.

---

[37] Psalm 118:24 ESV and Proverbs 27:1 ESV

Getting started is always the hardest part. Just like moving a parked car, the initial push takes the most effort, but once momentum begins, it rolls easier. Take one small step today. No matter how tiny. Decisions don't count if they don't translate into movement. Action is what starts the inertia. Energy expenditure is the cost for escaping the tomorrow trap. And it must be paid today.

The Cost of NOT Doing It

The cost of not fulfilling one's purpose is far greater than most people realize. Spiritually, it often shows up as a quiet emptiness, a lingering unrest or sense of being out of alignment with God's design. Emotionally, it can surface as dissatisfaction, restlessness, or the weight of unresolved what ifs that never fully go away. Relationally, missed purpose limits the impact you were meant to have on the people, communities, and even generations God placed within your reach. Practically, it can mean wasted time, unused gifts, and resources poured into pursuits that don't produce lasting or eternal significance.

When people reach the end of their lives and finally gain clarity, unfulfilled purpose becomes painfully visible. Hospice nurse Bronnie Ware, in *The Top Five Regrets of the Dying*, recorded what people most often expressed in their final days. The number one regret was this: "I wish I'd had the courage to live a life true to myself, not the life others expected of me." That regret isn't about missed vacations or career titles. It's about abandoning one's calling to meet expectations, avoid conflict, or seek approval. By the time the noise fades, what remains is the truth they wish they had honored sooner.

Of all human emotions, I dare say that regret and shame may be the heaviest to carry. Grief comes close, but time often softens grief; whereas regret and shame, if left unaddressed, can compound like interest.

But the greatest cost of all for not fulfilling our purpose is eternal perspective. One day, every life will stand before the throne of God, not to be compared with others, but to be measured against what could have been. The sobering thought isn't judgment alone; it's the realization of how far off the mark we may have lived from the life God intended for us. Seeing the purpose designed for you and recognizing how little of it was embraced is a cost no success, comfort, or excuse can outweigh.

LIVING FIT
FOR PURPOSE

Becoming fit for purpose is a lifelong endeavor because we never fully arrive. God always has something more for us.

Living fit for purpose is the life you continually walk out. Each day is another opportunity to stay aligned, to remain available, and to step into what God has prepared next. What got you here won't be enough for where you're going. There will always be new levels, new challenges, and new assignments. New seasons require new disciplines, so training never stops and refinement is continuous.

Living for purpose is not about *running for your life,* chasing quick wins, being reactive to every starting gun, and never following a consistent course. But it's about *running your life* with an intentional pursuit of purpose.

As you progress along your route, assemble guardrails to keep from drifting back into old patterns. Stay disciplined and avoid complacency.

New challenges are not setbacks; they are upgrades. The same discipline, awareness, and faith that brought you here will continue to carry you forward as you grow stronger, wiser, and more equipped. Stay rooted, stay focused, and keep moving forward with intention.

Part of living for purpose is leaving a legacy that points others in the right direction. You are always modeling something, and others are always watching and following. Pouring into the next generation is a way to multiply purpose through people. Think beyond yourself. Live with eternal impact in mind.

Sometimes living for purpose means carrying the light, not just for yourself, but for others who need it. Like the torchbearers in the Olympic Games, who run their leg of the race to pass the flame forward, we are called to carry what God has placed in us and deliver it where it's needed next. Even in nature, scientists have observed that ash from a super volcano can travel miles through the air before settling and then reignite into lava. What looks like something distant and scattered can still carry fire within it. In the same way, you may be called to move, to go, to carry the presence and truth of God into places you didn't expect, becoming the vessel that transports His light. Sometimes you are the flame, and sometimes you are the one carrying it, but either way, your role is essential in ensuring that the fire continues to spread.

At the end of it all, this life will not be measured by how busy you were, how much you accumulated, or how impressive things looked on the outside. It will be measured by whether you became who God created you to be and fulfilled what He placed in your hands.

You were not made to drift, to wander, or to settle for less; you were designed, trained, and refined for a purpose that only you can carry.

Stand up, step forward, and live it fully, boldly, and without hesitation. Stay aligned, stay ready, and stay faithful, because the time you have matters, the calling on your life is real, and what you do with it will echo far beyond you.

NOTE FROM THE AUTHOR

I hope you've enjoyed reading *Fit for Purpose* as much as I've enjoyed writing it. My heart behind these pages is that something within them stirred, challenged, or strengthened you in a meaningful way, whether that's in your faith, your mindset, your daily walk, or all combined. This journey of becoming fit for purpose is one we're all on together, and I'm grateful you chose to spend part of that journey here with me.

If this book impacted you, I'd truly appreciate you taking a moment to leave a review. Your feedback not only encourages me, but it also helps others discover the message and decide if it's something they need in their own season. Thank you for your time, your support, and for being part of this community.

ABOUT THE AUTHOR

Beyr Reyes is Jenny Minigh's pen name for the Christian genre.

Jenny received her doctorate degree in biomedical science. She has produced over 250 publications in science, medicine, and fiction genres. In addition, she has worked in the drug industry since 2005 as a regulatory writer for major international pharmaceutical and biotech companies.

OTHER BOOKS BY THE AUTHOR

Subject Your Flesh: And Stop Being a Victim of Your Destructive Desires
Beyr Reyes

Need to get control of your life? Tired of constant dieting? Fed up with bad habits? Subjection is the answer that lasts. Learn how to eradicate the problem areas in your life. Take control of your flesh and turn your life around using the Word of God.

2014 CSPA eBook of the Year

Make a Choice
Beyr Reyes

What do you believe and how do you show it? This book checks your foundational beliefs and then challenges you to uphold them. Make a choice and stand for what you believe in!

Readers Favorite 2011 Silver Award

Fast Answers: Fasting Plans for Specific Prayer Needs
Beyr Reyes

Want to try fasting but don't know where to start? This book had 1-, 3-, and 7-day fasts mapped out for you. Give it a try!

Taming Your MONSTER Appetite: Find a Healthy Lifestyle You Can Live With
Jennifer Minigh

It's time to deal with the appetite monsters in your life and get rid of stinkin' thinkin' that plagues your efforts to live a healthier lifestyle. Learn how to stand up and face your appetite monster head on.

489: A Short Story About Forgiveness
Beyr Reyes

If God gave you only 490 chances, what number would you be on? CSPA 2016 Fiction Book of the Year. A powerful story loaded with plot twists and emotion.

2016 CSPA Fiction Book of the Year

The Big Picture
Beyr Reyes

For the beginner, this book is a broad perspective of the Bible that will help to place events and their purposes. For the reader who usually goes deep, this book is a refreshing step back to illuminate the big picture.
Readers Favorite 2011 Bronze Award

Relaying the Word: A 16-Week Trek Through the Bible With Friends
Beyr Reyes

Never read the Bible? Or have read it lots of times? Either way, this small group bible study will bring fresh revelation and closer friends.

A Million Different Yous: A Short Story About Becoming Whole
Beyr Reyes

Being pulled in a million different directions? Overwhelmed with all you need to be? Read this powerful story how Rachael got herself together.

Renewable Energy: A Short Story About Second Chances
Beyr Reyes

Caught in a cosmic battle for "soular" energy, will Kane find his purpose? A twist on the history of mankind through the eyes of a fallen soul.